Celestial Walk

A DAILY JOURNEY
IN PRACTICAL INTIMACY

SUSAN ROLAND

outskirts
press

This book is dedicated to
my Lord and Savior.

I will declare Your lovingkindness in the morning
and Your faithfulness at night.

I also thank my dear husband
and three precious daughters.

When life has thrown me curves
and I've been tempted to despair,
you have given me courage to look up instead,
leaning on Him and fixing my eyes on the things above.

Table of Contents

Celestial Walk
365 Days of
Leaning on Him

One of the disciples, the one Jesus loved dearly,
was reclining against Him,
his head on His shoulder.
John 13:23 The Message

If there is one theme in this calendar, it is dependence on God. I love the thought of John, the beloved disciple, leaning on his Master. It's a position of trust, love, and dependence. That's what I long for with my Lord! I pray the Lord Jesus will draw you through this tool to cuddle against Him, your head on His shoulder, and put your full confidence in Him. My desire for you as you go through these daily meditations is that you would lean upon Jesus and that your character and priorities will grow to reflect His own.

Many of the entries you will read in this book were written during the sixteen years my husband and I were serving as missionaries in Costa Rica. During eight of those years we owned Celeste, our Harlequin Great Dane. Every morning I would take my prayer walk with Celeste and dedicate that time to prayer, calling it my Celestial Walk. In this book I invite you to join me each day as we take a Celestial Walk together.

The book includes a reading for each day of the week and enough entries to take you through a full calendar year. You may begin reading at any time of year. Take time to figure out where Lent and Advent fall in your current calendar year (just Google it!), and use either the Lent or Advent appendix for those dates. Be sure to keep track of where you left off so you can return there at the end of those special seasons.

Each day's meditation includes a short Bible passage to read slowly and intentionally. Let the Word soak in. Remind yourself of the short, scriptural thoughts throughout your day. My desire is not that you remember *my* words, but *His!* All scripture is taken from the New International Version, unless otherwise noted.

You may notice a passage or two that is used more than once in the year. That's ok. I often read a passage more than once in the year and learn new things!

My dad once said to me, "We become like what we worship." Join me in longing to become like Him!

SUNDAY
THE UNTRODDEN WAY
Reading of the Day: Joshua 3:1-8

"Then you will know which way to go, since you
have never been this way before…
Consecrate yourselves, for tomorrow the LORD
will do amazing things among you."
Joshua 3:4-5

What unseen difficulties lie the long,
dark mile of the untrodden way,
Oh, how our hearts hesitate to venture on
to the uncertainty of the unproven.
—Author Unknown

You've reached the end of the old year and the start
of the new. Somehow these milestones evoke a
certain response within our hearts. Behind you is
a known journey; before you, an untrodden way.
Joshua 3 bids you to surrender unreservedly in the
year ahead. You may be optimistic, or you might
be dreading another year. As you face the unknown
with renewed consecration, you can know that as
you trust in Him, God will lead the way.

Let's not pitch our tent and take our ease, but instead, with surrender,

Let us go forward with the banners flying,
to the high adventure of another year,
For we have not come this way before.
—George H. Morrison

MONDAY
SPILLING OVER
Reading of the Day: Colossians 2:1-7

"So then, just as you received Christ Jesus as Lord,
continue to live in him, rooted and built up in
him, strengthened in the faith as you were taught,
and overflowing with thankfulness."
Colossians 2:6-7

When you are bumped, what spills out?

Make this your prayer right now:

Lord, I pray that today I might continue by faith.
Looking back, it seems like putting my trust in You for
salvation was an awful lot easier than living by faith
in the here and now. Help me today to grow deeper
roots and be built up in my faith. May I continue to
learn today and every day You give me until I see You
face to face. And when I am bumped during the day,
may my cup be so full of Your grace, that only thank-
fulness will spill over.

TUESDAY
THE EXIGENCIES OF THE TIMES
Reading of the Day: I Timothy 6:11-16

What do George Washington, Helen Keller and the Apostle Paul have in common?

*I am only one, but still I am one. I cannot
do everything, but still I can do something;
and because I cannot do everything, I will not refuse
to do something that I can do.*
—Helen Keller

*We must never despair; our situation
has been compromising before,
and it has changed for the better.
If difficulties arise, we must put forth new exertion
and proportion our efforts
to the exigencies of the times.*
—George Washington

Flee…pursue…fight…take hold.
—Paul

All three quotes above touch upon the character quality of persistence. To fight the good fight, we must flee from temptation, pursue godliness, and take hold of the life to which God has called us. God will give you the strength to persist in proportion to the *exigencies of the times*. (I challenge you to use *that* phrase in the context of your day today!)

WEDNESDAY
SHORTCUT TO FAITH
Reading of the Day: Psalm 92:1-5

No, of course, there is no shortcut to faith! But as Ruth Myers wrote in her book, *31 Days of Praise*, "When in one way or another we slip off the freeway of faith, praise is often the ramp that gets us back on."

Praise either leads to victory that changes our circumstances, or gives us victory in the midst of circumstances that don't change. Praise is both a way of expressing our faith and of growing our faith. We see throughout Scripture that God is looking for our praise.

> "It is good to praise the Lord
> and make music to your name, O Most High,
> proclaiming your love in the morning
> and your faithfulness at night…"
> Psalm 92:1-2

Take time to write a note, and post it in a conspicuous place, reminding yourself to proclaim His unfailing love in the morning and His faithfulness in the evening.

THURSDAY
AT LEAST PRAY!
Reading of the Day: Genesis 24:10-26

"Before they call, I will answer;
while they are still speaking I will hear."
Isaiah 65:24

When Abraham sent his servant to find a wife for Isaac, the servant prayed for God to show lovingkindness to his master by answering a specific prayer to reveal the right choice.

"Before he had finished praying, Rebekah came out with her jar on her shoulder."
Genesis 24:15

Some days we need reminders that God is good for His word, that prayer makes a difference. Will God answer before we finish speaking if we never start speaking?!?

Take your concerns to God today. Don't just worry about them or shelve them. Pray about them! While you are still speaking, He will hear!

FRIDAY
DON'T GIVE UP!
Reading of the Day: Daniel 7:23-28

Daniel 7:25 speaks of Satan's strategy. "He will speak against the Most High and oppress his saints." The word *oppress* literally means to wear out. One of Satan's effective schemes is to wear out God's people. He uses exhaustion and profound discouragement to persuade us to give up opposing him.

Satan might wear out your human strength, but he cannot wear out the Holy Spirit's! Call on God's supernatural strength today to fight the good fight of faith and persist in proclaiming Christ. Colossians 1:29 says, "To this end I labor, struggling with all his energy, which so powerfully works in me." You have "all surpassing power" in your "jar of clay."
(2 Corinthians 4:7)

Call on God today to fill you with this power—the power that raised our Savior from the dead!

DON'T GIVE UP!

SATURDAY
TASTE OF HEAVEN
Reading of the Day: Colossians 3:1-4

My husband and I won't ever forget our dearly loved Great Dane, Celeste. I'll be mentioning her quite often in my devotional thoughts.

Each and every morning, as I would take time to walk and pray on my "Celestial Walk," she had one passion. She kept her eyes and mind on the things above, focusing on any movement in the treetops, longing to see a squirrel. Only once did Celeste actually get the taste of squirrel in her mouth. She savored the fleeting moment before the squirming creature managed to escape!

May even our smallest taste of heaven keep us looking at the things above!

"Set your minds on things above,
not on earthly things.
For you died, and your life is now hidden with
Christ in God."
Colossians 3:2-3

SUNDAY
SATISFIED!
Reading of the Day: Genesis 25:5-11

Our oldest daughter, Norma, taught our grand-kids to say "I'm satisfied" when they'd had enough to eat. Once, after several hours at the Chicago Aquarium, young Adrian announced to me, "I'm satisfied with fish!"

It's hard to be content. Matt Atkins wrote, "The problem with contentment is that I always want more of it." Paul wrote about being content whether in need or in plenty. Being satisfied doesn't come naturally. In fact, it's a proof there is something beyond what life on earth has to offer. Pray today that you might live up to Abraham's epitaph:

> "Abraham breathed his last and
> died in a ripe old age,
> an old man and satisfied with life..."
> Genesis 25:8a NASB

PS: Adrian, keep living a life of being satisfied with God!

MONDAY
SUSTAINED BY HIS HAND
Reading of the Day: Isaiah 46:1-4

Isaiah 46 starts out by drawing a picture of the famous idols of Babylon being carted off into exile along with this once-powerful nation. The fantastic images created by their hands are now prey to their enemies.

> "They stoop and bow down together;
> unable to rescue the burden,
> they themselves go off into captivity."
> Isaiah 46:2

In great contrast, God calls attention to His people, "You whom I have upheld since you were conceived, and have carried since your birth… I have made you and I will carry you; I will sustain you and I will rescue you." (vss. 3,4)

The Babylonians and their man-made idols were helpless. But God's people, formed by His own hand, were sustained and rescued by God Himself. You, too, are God's creation today, sustained by His hand.

TUESDAY
HELPLESSNESS PLUS FAITH
Reading of the Day: I Peter 5:1-11

"Cast all your anxiety on Him,
because He cares for you."
I Peter 5:7

Helplessness united with faith produces prayer.
—O. Hallesby

Don't let your helplessness drive you to anxiety but to God. Faith is simply going to Christ with your helplessness. Think on what things today might make you feel fearful or anxious. Psalm 34:4 says, "I sought the Lord, and He answered me, and delivered me from all my fears."

Fear and anxiety can be significant motivating forces. Turn them into positive motivators. As you seek God at your point of fear, look for specific promises that can transform your fear responses into faith responses. Strive to form the habit of immediately taking your helplessness to Him. Or, as Amy Carmichael wrote, "Turn on the instant."

WEDNESDAY
A STRANGELY PERSISTENT "I"
Reading of the Day: Philippians 2:1-11

Amy Carmichael wrote that even after fully committing her life to God in the morning, often "a strangely persistent **I** can rise up suddenly."

My dear friend and e-mentor, Win Couchman, once challenged me to set high goals in marriage. After praying and struggling over that challenge for a week, I called her back to ask what her own high goals included. One of them was simply, "Eliminate selfishness." Wow! That is a high goal, indeed!

Take a moment right now to fully commit your life to God. Then ask Him to help you recommit yourself several times during the day. Recall the song "Turn Your *Eyes* Upon Jesus." Think of that song during the day, remembering to turn your *"I's"* over to him, not just your **eyes**!

THURSDAY
DESPAIR V. TRUST
Reading of the Day: John 20:24-29

"Stop being an unbeliever and believe."
John 20:27b

I hit a crisis point one night. I'd been dealing with pain, nausea, and depression for several weeks after a difficult surgery. It was a long and somewhat questionable recovery. I was alone, sitting up wide awake in our recliner in the middle of the night. I was tempted to despair and was praying honestly about it. As I talked to God, I realized I had just two options: despair or trust. As I considered the first, I thought, "Despair has absolutely nothing to offer me." So, I asked God's help to choose the only logical option: TRUST.

I think those are the two options Thomas also faced. Jesus put it clearly to him, "Stop being an unbeliever and believe." It all boils down to that!

You and I don't have the resurrected Jesus at our side, giving us the choice between the two while inviting us to thrust our hand in His side. Thomas' choice is the same one you and I face. Though we can't enjoy His physical presence at our sides, we have a blessing not offered to Thomas: "Blessed are those who have not seen and yet have believed." (John 20:29b)

Choose trust today!

FRIDAY
"BUT HE DESERVED IT!"
Reading of the Day: Philippians 1:27-29

"Be kind and compassionate to one another,
forgiving each other,
just as in Christ God forgave you."
Ephesians 4:32

I'm never more tempted to be rude than when someone deserves it. Think about that for a minute. Should you treat someone rudely if they *deserve* it? What do *you* deserve? And if you treat them as *they* deserve, are you following God's guideline to conduct yourself in a manner *worthy* of the gospel?

(Ouch!)

If anyone crosses your path today who seems to deserve an unkind response, ask God to help you be kind, tenderhearted, and forgiving. If you resist that initial, uncaring response, someone just might see Jesus in you!

SATURDAY
CELESTIAL WALK, PART I: WORSHIP
Reading of the Day: I Kings 8:22-30

Over the next few days, join me on my "Celestial Walk." On my daily prayer walks, I first focus on worship. Harold Best says that worship is, "…acknowledging that someone or something else is… worth more, and by consequence, to be obeyed, feared, and adored…Worship is the sign that in giving myself completely to someone or something, I want to be mastered by it."

Warren Wiersbe says, "Worship is the believer's response of all that they are—mind, emotions, will, body—to what God is and says and does."

As I walk, I begin with an attitude of worship:

"Lord, the God of Israel, there is no God like you in heaven above or on earth below—you who keep your covenant of love with your servants who continue wholeheartedly in your way."
I Kings 8:23

Our Great Dane used to accompany me on my walk each morning in Costa Rica. Celeste was confident there was no one like me. She found joy in walking before me with all her heart! Let's live out our confidence in God in the same "Celestial" way, starting out our day with worship.

SUNDAY
CELESTIAL WALK PART II: POETRY PRAYER
Reading of the Day: John 13:21-30

As I continue my Celestial Walk, I pray a poem by Amy Carmichael.

Make this your prayer today:

As John upon his dear Lord's breast,
so would I lean, so would I rest.
As empty shell in depths of sea,
so would I sink, be filled with Thee.

As water lily in her pool through long,
hot hours is still and cool,
A thought of peace, so I would be thy water lily,
close by Thee.

As singing bird in high blue air,
so would I soar and sing Thee there.
Nor rain nor stormy wind can be,
when all the air is full of Thee.

And so, though daily duties crowd and
dust of earth be like a cloud,
Through noise of words, O Lord, my Rest,
thy John would lean upon Thy breast.

MONDAY
CELESTIAL WALK, PART III:
CONFESSION
Reading of the Day: Psalm 6

Let's continue our prayer walk, taking a moment for confession.

Make the following Scripture your personal prayer:

> "Lord, do not rebuke me in your anger
>   or discipline me in your wrath.
> Have mercy on me, Lord, for I am faint;
> heal me, Lord, for my bones are in agony.
>   My soul is in deep anguish.
>   How long, Lord, how long?"
>   Psalm 6:1-3

I willingly lay bare my heart before You today. I ask You to reveal my sins, weaknesses, and handicaps and help me to be unashamed to confess them. I confess my dependence on You today to break wrong habits, practices, and ways of life. Help me to look self-stuff straight in the face, nail it to the cross, and accept Your forgiveness. In His grace-filled name, Amen.

TUESDAY
CELESTIAL WALK, PART IV:
CHANGE MY HEART!
Reading of the Day: II Corinthians 3:7-18

Deuteronomy 10:16 says, "Change your hearts and stop being stubborn." Often our stubborn souls not only refuse to change, but refuse to even recognize the *need* for change. It's easy to see how other people's lives need transformation. Instead, God calls on us to put our own stubbornness away and ask for a change of heart.

"And we all, who with unveiled faces contemplate the Lord's glory, are being transformed into his image with ever-increasing glory, which comes from the Lord, who is the Spirit."
II Corinthians 3:18

Ask God to reveal to you any specific way in which He wants to change you. Jot it down and pray daily for His Spirit to work in you to effect that change through His power. He will honor your persistent prayer!

WEDNESDAY
CELESTIAL WALK, PART V:
SPIRITUAL RENEWAL
Reading of the Day: II Chronicles 15:10-15

I ask you to join me today in the portion of my Celestial Walk where I pray for spiritual renewal. Take your time as you pray through each word and phrase below.

> *Give me a heart full of fire for Your Son,*
> *igniting the whole of*
> *my heart, soul, mind and strength.*
> *Thrill me with Your Word.*
> *I give you my time, health, energy, strength, tongue,*
> *thoughts, emotions, attitudes, priorities, resources,*
> *relationships, passions, needs, and desires.*

"Love the LORD your God with all your heart
and with all your soul and with all your strength."
Deuteronomy 6:5

THURSDAY
CELESTIAL WALK, PART VI:
PETITION
Reading of the Day: Philippians 4:4-9

Sometimes we feel guilty about bringing so many requests to God. But what decent father is upset when his daughter comes before him with the concerns of her heart, asking her dad for help? Even so, petition is an important part of prayer, as long as we are not like whining kids at the grocery store check-out!

Take a moment to really think through and talk to God about whatever is on your mind. What are any special concerns you have today? Talk to Him about your activities of the day (Plan A), and confess to Him your willingness to accept and honor Him if He chooses a Plan B instead.

> "Do not be anxious about anything,
> but in everything,
> by prayer and petition, with thanksgiving,
> present your requests to God."
> Philippians 4:6

FRIDAY
CELESTIAL WALK, PART VII:
INTERCESSION
Reading of the Day: I Samuel 12:18-25

How would God want us to intercede for one another?

Frank Laubach writes, *"One need not tell God everything about the people for whom one prays. Holding them one by one steadily before the mind and willing*

that God may have His will with them is the best, for
God knows better than we what our friends need, yet
our prayer releases His power."

"As for me, far be it from me that I should sin
against the LORD by failing to pray for you."
I Samuel 12:23

In today's Bible reading, the people beg Samuel
to intercede for them. He could have asked many
things, but his plea is that they would serve the
Lord with all their hearts. As you pray for others,
ask God to open your eyes so that you may see that
person as God does, and pray for what He might
desire for them.

SATURDAY
ROSES AND THORNS
Reading of the Day: Luke 24:13-27

As Jesus walked alongside the men on the road to
Emmaus, He asked them, "What have you been
discussing together?" I would give an arm and a leg
to just have one afternoon to leisurely walk with
Jesus at my side and have Him ask me what I happen to be thinking about!

You've been accompanying me each morning on my
Celestial Walk. Now I invite you to join me on my
afternoon walk, which I call "Roses and Thorns."

I used to walk through the tropical paradise just outside our door in Costa Rica. I would stop to smell the roses – both literally and figuratively. On this walk, I would let Celeste lead me wherever she wanted to wander, and I would take in the beauty around me as I talked to God about the roses and thorns of my day.

We must be intentional to recognize the roses with which God graces our lives. At the same time, I believe He is also glorified when we are honest about the thorns and take them directly to Him. Take a moment now to talk to God about the roses and thorns of your day.

> *If I cannot unfold a rosebud,*
> *This flower of God's design,*
> *How can I have wisdom to*
> *Unfold this life of mine?*
> —Anonymous

> "Cast all your anxiety on him
> because he cares for you."
> I Peter 5:7

SUNDAY
MIRRORING GOD'S MOURNING
Reading of the Day: John 11:33-37 and
Luke 19:37-44

"Jesus wept." John 11:35

I'm thankful for the challenge in my childhood to memorize Scripture. We often kidded about John 11:35 being the easiest verse in the Bible to memorize. A few years ago, I finally began to consider that verse very seriously.

Jesus also wept earlier as He looked over the city of Jerusalem. As the crowds (and even the disciples) were in a frenzy of joy, welcoming the King, Jesus wept over the condition of their hearts.

How often do we celebrate enthusiastically while God weeps over a lost people, longing for us to join Him in His sorrow? As Gary Thomas wrote, "Joy without occasional mourning is naiveté, not wisdom."

Are your heart's emotions and priorities in tune with God's today?

MONDAY
TOUGH PHRASE OF THE DAY:
MOST GLADLY
Reading of the Day: II Corinthians 12:1-10

And He has said to me, "My grace is sufficient for
you, for power is perfected in weakness.
most gladly, therefore,
I will rather boast about my weaknesses,
so that the power of Christ may dwell in me."
II Corinthians 12:9 NASB

It's easy to talk about being happy to be weak so
that God's power might dwell in us. But when I
truly feel at my weakest and most vulnerable, I find
that phrase difficult. Even at my weakest, people
have often told me that I am so strong. But I know
I am not! It requires effort and God's grace to im-
plement the phrase, "most gladly!" It does not come
naturally—at least to me!

God shows His strength in the weak.
Those of us who are weak must rely on Him with all
our hearts, and God loves us because of it.
—Esther Ahn Kim

Impress on your mind right now the phrase:

"MOST GLADLY!"

TUESDAY
TOUGH PHRASE OF THE DAY: WELL CONTENT
Reading of the Day:
Re-read II Corinthians 12:1-10 SLOWLY

Let's add another tough phrase to yesterday's "**most gladly**."

> "Therefore I am *well content* with weaknesses,
> with insults, with distresses, with persecutions,
> with difficulties, for Christ's sake;
> for when I am weak, then I am strong."
> II Corinthians 12:9-10 NASB

Make this your prayer today:

*Lord, when I hit the wall of uncertainty, inadequacy, frustration, weakness, difficulties, and pain today, help me remember to **most gladly** confess my need of You and my dependence upon You. Help me to be **well content** with the circumstances and limitations You have allowed. I know You can show Your power through them and through me.*

Keep in mind two phrases today: "**most gladly**" and "**well content**."

WEDNESDAY
FOOLING OURSELVES
Reading of the Day: Luke 6:27-36

Sometimes we fool ourselves by thinking people will know we are Christians and will want to know more about Jesus just because we are nice. (And we're not even always that nice!) There are a lot of nice people who don't know Christ. As Francis Chan puts it, "There has to be more to our faith than friendliness, politeness, and even kindness."

> "If you love those who love you,
>   what credit is that to you?
> Even sinners love those who love them."
>   Luke 6:32

The thing that really bewilders the world is when we *love our enemies*. "True faith is loving a person after he has hurt you. True love makes you stand out."

Who are the people you avoid or who avoid you? Who are the people who have hurt you or your friends or your kids? Are you willing to love them today? They will know you are a Christian by your love!

THURSDAY
TRANSFORMED!
Reading of the Day: I Peter 2:4-10

"But you are a chosen people, a royal priesthood, a holy nation, God's special possession, that you may declare the praises of him who called you out of darkness into his wonderful light."
I Peter 2:9

He maketh the rebel a priest and a king
He hath bought us and taught us this new song to sing
Unto Him who hath lov'd us and wash'd us from sin
Unto Him be the glory forever! Amen!

Think back to what you once were and where you might be today if it weren't for His grace. Thank Him that He transformed you into a priest and a king. If you have the chance, sing the above hymn to the tune of "Immortal, Invisible, God Only Wise."

Remember today: you are a rebel turned priest and king!

FRIDAY
THIS MOMENT WILL NEVER RETURN
Reading of the Day: I Thessalonians 5:12-24

Amy Carmichael wrote, "So let us praise Him now, though it may be from under the harrow, from the depths, from anywhere." You will never again have a chance to return to this moment or these circumstances to praise Him. If you don't love Him right now with contentment, this moment will never return to give you that chance.

"Give thanks in all circumstances,
for this is God's will for you in Christ Jesus."
I Thessalonians 5:18

What would you become like if you took advantage of every single trial and tribulation to praise Him and rest in His peace of great contentment? You would certainly become much more like your Savior! Pray right now that God would allow you to respond with praise and contentment in the opportunities today presents.

SATURDAY
TRUST TO ASPIRE TO!
Reading of the Day: II Kings 18:1-8

"Hezekiah trusted in the LORD, the God of Israel.
There was no one like him among all the kings of
Judah, either before him or after him."
2 Kings 18:5-6

Sometimes you hear someone jokingly refer to the book of Hezekiah in the Bible. Though there is no such book, King Hezekiah probably deserved a book of the Bible named in his honor. The most outstanding quality about him was his trust in the Lord. He trusted God like no king before or after him.

That's a level of trust to aspire to! Remember that others will be impacted as they observe how much your trust in God makes a difference in your day.

SUNDAY
5 DECLARATIONS OF BELIEF
Reading of the Day: Hebrews 10:19-25

Beth Moore has challenged me to be more of a woman of faith. I've memorized her thoughts on belief and ask you to declare them today as true in your own life.

   * God is who He says He is.
   * God can do what He says He can do.
   * I am who God says I am.
   * I can do all things through Christ.
   * God's Word is alive and active in me.

> "I can do everything through him
> who gives me strength."
> Philippians 4:13

MONDAY
GODLY IMPULSES
Reading of the Day: John 21:1-8

"He said, 'Throw your net on the right side of the
boat and you will find some.'
When they did, they were unable to haul the net
in because of the large number of fish.
Then the disciple whom Jesus loved said to Peter,
'It is the Lord!'
As soon as Simon Peter heard him say, 'It is the Lord,'
he wrapped his outer garment around him (for he
had taken it off) and jumped into the water."
John 21:6-7

Peter's sudden impulses sometimes got him into
trouble. But, sometimes they served him well —
like when he swam to Jesus with all his might.

Prayer for today:

God, put Your truth deep into me,
reaching parts I don't even realize exist.
So fill me with Your Spirit that even my reactions
and sudden impulses are godly.

TUESDAY
SERVICE AND SACRIFICE
Reading of the Day: John 21:15-19

"I tell you the truth, when you were younger you
dressed yourself and went where you wanted;
but when you are old you will stretch out your
hands, and someone else will dress you
and lead you where you do not want to go."
John 21:18

Life seems to fall into two categories:

- Going where you want to go—service

    and

- Going where you do not want to
  go—sacrifice

Jesus followed the above declaration with the command, "Follow Me!" No matter which category you fall into today, follow Him!

WEDNESDAY
SNUGGLING WITH GOD
Reading of the Day: Isaiah 54:5-10

I love snuggling up with my grandchildren!! There's nothing quite as precious as cuddling up on the couch together, watching *Toy Story* or reading a book.

God loves to snuggle with us, too. When we were living for 12 years in Bolivia as well as for 16 years in Costa Rica, every day I used to look out my window at the mountains and was reminded,

> "Though the mountains be shaken
> and the hills be removed,
> yet my unfailing love for you will not be shaken."
> Isaiah 54:10

Have you ever seen how much time and effort it takes to cut a road through a small segment of mountain? After weeks on end of dynamite blasting, earth movers, and bulldozers, finally there is enough mountain chipped away to put a short segment of road through.

If one could move a hill, or even an entire mountain, God's love for you would not be shaken. Cuddle up to Him today!

THURSDAY
SOARING LIKE EAGLES
Reading of the Day: Isaiah 40:21-31

> "He gives strength to the weary and
> increases the power of the weak.
> Even youths grow tired and weary,
> and young men stumble and fall;
> but those who hope in the LORD

will renew their strength.
They will soar on wings like eagles;
they will run and not grow weary,
they will walk and not be faint."
Isaiah 40:29-31

Prayer for today:

Lord, give me a sense of wonder and hope and imagination and vision; eyes to see what You are up to! Give me an ability to dream today. You are an awesome Creator! Nothing is impossible for You. You can forgive and cleanse me and start a new work in me. You can enable Me to rise above the pull of sin's weight. You can help me soar on wings like an eagle—in victory, in ongoing obedience, in steadfastness of spirit, and in fruitful ministry.

Amen

FRIDAY
CHANGE OF HEART
Reading of the Day:
Habakkuk 1:1-6 and 3:17-19

Have you ever noticed the change in Habakkuk from the early passages to the later ones? In chapter 1, verse 2 he cries out, "How long, O Lord, must I call for help, but you do not listen?"

I love some of the final verses:

"Though the fig tree does not bud...
and the olive crop fails...
yet I will rejoice in the Lord,
I will be joyful in God my Savior."

It's interesting that in reply to Habakkuk's heartfelt cry, God did not offer soothing words. Instead, in chapter 1, verses 5 and 6, He described how He would allow even more destruction.

God seemed more interested in truth than in making Habakkuk feel better. God drew Habakkuk's attention to Himself and to His long-range plans and asked two things of him:

1) live by faith and 2) wait for revelation.

Instead of changing his circumstances, God changed his heart. Perhaps He wants to do that in your life today?

SATURDAY
JUST SAY IT!
Reading of the Day: Psalm 42

It seems that a lot of Christians don't realize God can handle honesty. We like to address God as we think we ought to speak, and often our words outrun our thoughts. A.W. Tozer wrote that it is best to be perfectly frank before Him. "He will allow us to say anything we will, so long as it is to Himself."

> "I say to God my Rock,
> 'Why have you forgotten me?'"
> Psalm 42:9a

Wouldn't it have impressed us more if the Psalmist had cried out, "Lord, thou canst not forget! Thou hast graven my name on the palms of thy hands." Which prayer do you think God preferred? Perhaps the second sounds worthier. Surely the first more truly expressed his feelings.

Take a moment right now to be perfectly frank before God.

SUNDAY
UTTERLY HONEST
Reading of the Day: Jeremiah 20:7-18; 21:1

Continuing yesterday's theme, David M'Intyre wrote, "Honest dealing becomes us when we kneel in His pure presence."

Superficiality and artificiality seep into our very blood, contaminating our thoughts, attitudes, and relationships. There was nothing that raised Christ's dander more than hypocrisy. A.W. Tozer wrote, "Prayer will increase in power and reality as we repudiate all pretense and learn to be utterly honest before God as well as before men."

Jeremiah cried out, "O LORD, you deceived me, and I was deceived!" What terrible words to utter before Him who is changeless truth! But the prophet spoke as he felt, and despite it, the Lord met him and continued to speak to him and through him.

Be frank before God, and let Him meet you where you are.

MONDAY
NO FEAR!
Reading of the Day: Joshua 10:1-8

Joshua had plenty of reason to "fear greatly" when faced with five angry kings ready to destroy Gibeon. Yet God told him, "Do not fear them, for I have given them into your hands; not one of them shall stand before you." Verses 10 and 11 describe a "great wounding" and a great victory.

The famous series of Rocky movies were loosely based on the true story of Chuck Wepner. Chuck was best known for his fight against reigning boxing champion, Mohammed Ali. Nicknamed "The Bayonne Bleeder," he set the precedent for the character in Rocky getting hit again and again in the face. At the end of the ninth round in Wepner's fight with Ali, he scored a knockdown. In his corner between rounds, he told his manager, "Al, start the car. We're going to the bank. We're millionaires." In the remaining rounds he suffered cuts above both eyes and a broken nose before the ref called a technical knock-out.

Sometimes we choose to use the tactic of letting Satan hit us in the face again and again until we are called out of the fight. Fighting the good fight of faith requires all our strength and stamina. Many times, we invest our efforts instead in pity parties, resentment, anger, and unforgiveness.

Choose today to put your energy into the right fight.

> "Greater is He who is in you than
> he who is in the world."
> I John 4:4

TUESDAY
OUT OF CONTROL
Reading of the Day: Hebrews 11:1-7

I have had more than my share of endoscopies. I've had good ones and bad ones. I'm never sure which one was worse—the one in Bolivia with no anesthesia at all (i.e. "Take this garden hose and swallow it!")—or the time I had just enough anesthesia to be uncooperative. I hate the feeling of being out of control!

Yet faith means admitting we are not in control. "… being sure of what we hope for and certain of what we do not see." Abraham was a man of faith. He left all that was familiar— his home, his extended family, his culture. He clung to God's promise, even when its fulfillment seemed impossibly distant.

Is there some out-of-control element in your life today? Honor God by clinging to His faithfulness today, even when you don't know where you are going!

"And he went out, not knowing where he was going."
Hebrews 11:8

WEDNESDAY
NOT FROM AROUND HERE?
Reading of the Day: Hebrews 11:8-19

When you read the account of Abraham in Genesis, you might not come away impressed with his great faith. Yet in Hebrews 11, twelve verses are dedicated to his exemplary faith. Among the examples were his willingness to go, not knowing where; living as an alien in the land of promise; looking for a spiritual city, not one on earth; and offering up his son, believing that God could raise him from the dead.

An important element of a life of faith is recognizing *I'M NOT FROM HERE!*

Longing for another country makes God proud!

"Instead, they were longing for a better country—
a heavenly one.
Therefore God is not ashamed to be
called their God;
for He has prepared a city for them."
Hebrews 11:16

THURSDAY
TRIPPING AND WOBBLING
Reading of the Day: Hebrews 11:20-29

Make God proud of you today. Don't get too comfortable in this world!

Do you feel like your faith would never qualify you for the list in Hebrews 11? I doubt any of those listed there felt like they lived their lives well enough to be put on that list.

They may have tripped and wobbled along their race,
but they made it across the finish line having done
what they were called to do.
—Beth Moore in *The Patriarchs*

Today, make a pact to not make yourself too much at home on this earth.

"Let us hold unswervingly to the hope we profess,
for he who promised is faithful."
Hebrews 10:23

FRIDAY
WHAT KIND OF HEROES?
Reading of the Day: Hebrews 11: 30-40

Sometimes we think that victory over sickness and suffering is the outcome of remarkable faith. It's interesting to note the contrasts in today's Scripture reading. In fact, look at just one verse of the passage. Verse 35 says,

"Women received back their dead, raised to life again. There were others who were tortured, refusing to be released so that they might gain an even better resurrection."

Hebrews 11 is the roll call of people with exemplary faith. We have looked at a few that seemed like they might not quite qualify for that badge of honor. But overall, we can greatly admire and aspire to examples like Enoch, Abraham, Joseph, and Moses. It's inspiring to read about those who through faith conquered kingdoms, administered justice, and escaped the edge of the sword. Who doesn't want their "weakness turned to strength?" (v.34)

But on this list, commended for their faith, are those who were tortured, jeered, flogged, chained, destitute, and mistreated. Since faith is confidence in what we do not see, I think those who never saw victory on earth are at the top of the list as the big winners in the race of faith. If things are not going as you wish, choose to hope in the eternal promises, and put your faith in God Himself, and not what might seem like a positive outcome.

SATURDAY
GIVING WHEN IT HURTS
Reading of the Day: II Samuel 24:18-25

"I will not sacrifice to the Lord my
God burnt offerings
that cost me nothing." II Samuel 24:24b

Too often I am more than happy to serve God… if it doesn't cost me much!

Time and again we see biblical examples of faith being what one is willing to give up, *not* what one is able to coax God into! Abraham was a great man of faith, not because of his comfort and affluence, but because he was willing to obey God at a great cost.

Think about your prayer life. Do you spend much of your effort trying to talk God into doing what you want? Focus your prayers today on God's goodness and faithfulness. Praise Him, and profess confidence that He will equip you for every good work. Be still before Him, and listen to how He would have you obey. Be willing to give of yourself, even when it hurts.

SUNDAY
BIG PRAYERS
Jeremiah 32:16-26

"Ah, Sovereign LORD, you have made
the heavens and the earth
by your great power and outstretched arm.
Nothing is too hard for you."
Jeremiah 32:17

Some of the most awesome things God will ever do for you will come out of the most awful things in your life. There are a few "awful things" that have happened to me where the awesome outcomes are clear to me.

There are other awful things where the outcomes are still hazy to me. But I trust He knows the good that comes from them. I still have the perspective of looking at the back side of the tapestry. The Grand Weaver, though, sees the beautiful design on the front.

Join me today in preoccupying ourselves with believing God, rather than focusing on negative emotions. God loves big prayers! Let's pray BIG right now, using the verse above as a basis for our prayers.

MONDAY
BLESSED CONTROLLER
Reading of the Day: I Timothy 6:11-16

(If possible, read from *The New Testament in Modern English*, J. B. Phillips))

Whatever He permits or sends is an invitation to draw closer to Him.
—Ruth Myers

God is the blessed [warm, caring, generous, gracious] Controller of all things [working all things into a pattern of good for those who love Him].
I Timothy 6:15 J. B. Phillips Version
(plus Susan's comments!)

With God, nothing is accidental, nothing is incidental, and no experience is wasted.
—Anonymous

Repeat the above phrase several times to ingrain it in your thoughts. As life happens today, remember that nothing is accidental, nothing is incidental, and no experience is wasted in terms of eternity.

TUESDAY
NON-RIGHTS
Reading of the Day:
Look up the passages listed below

The world around you will constantly remind you of your rights.

Look at the Scriptures below to remind you of a few rights you *don't* have!

You *don't* have the right to:
1. Determine the motives of another. (Only God can see the heart. I Chronicles 28:9)
2. Think you are better than anyone else. (All have sinned. Romans 3:23)
3. Judge others. (God alone is Judge. Romans 14:10)
4. Be resentful. (God commands you to forgive. Matthew 18:21, 22)

Remind yourself of the rights you *don't* have. Jot them down on a note you'll see throughout the day. Which one of these might you be holding onto today as if it were *your* right?

WEDNESDAY
SPANISH PHRASE OF THE DAY:
"DIOS PRIMERO"
Reading of the Day: Acts 16:6-10

When future plans are unsure in Spanish you can say, "Dios primero," literally, "God first." It's a bit like James 4:15: "Instead, you ought to say, 'If the Lord, wills, [Dios primero], we will live and also do this or that.'"

Paul is a prime example of living "Dios primero." He made careful plans to visit Asia. "Let us return and visit the brethren in every city in which we proclaimed the word of the Lord, and see how they are." (Acts 15:36) As he was following through on these plans, "The Spirit of Jesus did not permit them [to go into Bithynia.]" (Acts 16:7) Later, when he saw the vision of the Macedonian appeal, he immediately changed plans. (Acts 16:9)

Make your plans today, but hold them loosely! Dios primero.

THURSDAY
ANTI-THEFT POLICY
Reading of the Day: Galatians 5:16-26

Each day we face spiritual battle as Christians. God longs for you to bear the fruit of the Spirit. The enemy longs to steal it. Pray today:

I am thankful that You have made a provision so that today
I can live filled with the Spirit of God demonstrating His presence through
> *Love, joy, and peace*
> *With long-suffering, gentleness, and goodness*
> *With meekness, faithfulness, and self-control in my life.*
I recognize that this is Your will for me, and therefore, with the power of the Holy Spirit,
I resist all the endeavors of the enemy to rob me of Your will for me today.

FRIDAY
ANTI-THEFT POLICY: CLAUSE 2
Reading of the Day: Romans 8:31-39

Continuing yesterday's theme of spiritual battle, remember today that God is fighting on your side. He is your ADT, Pinkerton's, and Brink's all rolled into one. He also has such great love for you that He has sacrificed *all* for you and desires to freely give you all good things.

> "What then shall we say to these things?
> If God is for us, who is against us?
> He who did not spare His own Son,

> but delivered Him over for us all,
> how will He not also with Him
> freely give us all things?"
> Romans 8:31-32

Prayer for today:

Lord, set me free to be everything You planned.
Don't let the enemy steal one bit of the victory You
have for me today.

SATURDAY
NO EXCLUSION CLAUSE
Reading of the Day: Matthew 4:17-20;
John 21:22-23

When Jesus was first interacting with His disciples, He had one principle message: "Follow me!"

Two of His very last words were, "Follow me!"

Perhaps we should lend great importance to these words, which were key from beginning to end of Jesus' ministry. Jesus adds the following chilling words to this command we often treat so lightly, "Whoever of you does not renounce all that he has cannot be my disciple." We tend to gloss over these words. They imply an inner surrender, with no exclusion causes.

To follow Christ, it is essential not only to repent of isolated sins, but, as John Stott wrote, to "renounce the very principle of self-will which lies at the root of every sin. To follow Christ is to surrender to him the rights over our own lives... [Jesus] does not call us to a sloppy half-heartedness, but to a vigorous, absolute commitment."

Pray about what exclusion clause you might need to delete from your own personal life policy that contradicts Jesus' sobering words, "Follow me!"

SUNDAY
BELIEVING THE BEST
Reading of the Day: II Corinthians 4:7-15

"For we who are alive are always being given over
to death for Jesus' sake,
so that his life may be revealed in our mortal body."
II Corinthians 4:11

Through problems and pain, I have become more aware of "being given over to death for Jesus' sake." * I pray that my losses might result in Jesus' life being revealed in my physical body as well as in my words, thoughts, attitudes, and behavior, in order to bring gain for Jesus' sake. God's reasons for allowing this are not trivial. I may never see the reasons, but I choose to walk by faith and believe the best of my Master.

Is there some way you are facing loss today? Recognize before God that His reasons for allowing this aren't trivial, and believe the best of your Master today.

* In the context of the above verse, "given over to death" does not necessarily refer to physical death. Otherwise, His life wouldn't be revealed in our mortal bodies!

MONDAY
THEOLOGY OF SUFFERING
Reading of the Day: Colossians 1:24-29

"Now I rejoice in what was suffered for you, and I fill up in my flesh what is still lacking in regard to Christ's afflictions, for the sake of his body, which is the church."
Colossians 1:24

I don't fully understand the theology of suffering. It is one of those secret things that won't be revealed to us until we see Him face to face. I *do* know the Bible speaks not only of Christ's afflictions but also "promises" again and again that we, too, will suffer if we choose to follow in the Master's footsteps.

On the eve of cancer surgery, John Piper wrote a convincing and convicting article called, "Don't Waste Your Cancer." He wrote that you will waste your cancer if

- You do not believe God designed it for you

- You believe it is a curse, not a gift

- You seek comfort from your odds rather than from God

- You believe that "beating cancer" means staying alive rather than cherishing Christ

- You grieve as those who have no hope

- You treat sin as casually as before

- You fail to use it as a witness to the truth and glory of Christ

You may not be facing a cancer diagnosis today. But, consider the above challenges as you face promised affliction.

TUESDAY
THAT I MAY KNOW HIM
Reading of the Day: Philippians 3:7-14

"That I may know Him, that I may become more
deeply and intimately acquainted with Him,
perceiving and recognizing and understanding
the wonders of His person more strongly
and more clearly."
Philippians 1:10a Amplified Version

May I know what I ought to know
Love what I ought to love

Praise what most pleases You
Value what is precious in Your eyes
And reject what You find vile.
—Thomas à Kempis

Take a moment to pray not only that God helps you to truly know Him, but also to grow in your *desire* to love and please Him.

WEDNESDAY
MISSING WORDS
Reading of the Day: Matthew 28:16-20

"Therefore go and make disciples of all nations, baptizing them in the name of the Father and of the Son and of the Holy Spirit, and teaching them everything I have commanded you.
And surely I am with you always, to the very end of the age."
Matthew 28:19-20

Once we were at a conference with about 200 missionaries gathered from all over the world. The above passage was shown to all of us on the big screen, and the speaker asked us, "What are the missing words?"

OK, don't cheat! Re-read the above cited passage and identify the missing words. If you don't catch them right away, you're in good company! Neither did about 90% of those in that audience!

Do you want to remain in Jesus' love? Then pay attention to the missing words!!

(Sorry, I won't give away the answer! Look it up in your own Bible and see what words I left out.)

THURSDAY
DON'T TRUST YOUR INTUITION
Reading of the Day: I John 1:5 - 2:6

Over the next few days I want to focus on Philippians 4:8:

> "Finally, brothers, *whatever is true*,
> whatever is noble, whatever is right,
> whatever is pure, whatever is lovely,
> whatever is admirable,
> if anything is excellent or praiseworthy—
> think about such things."

As you go through your day today, remember the phrase "whatever is true." Do my thoughts and words agree with the Bible? Are they free of deceit?

In her great book, *Loving God with All Your Mind*, Elizabeth George has challenged me to not trust my intuition as to what others are thinking or feeling. I think I have a pretty good record of intuiting. But just one or two misjudgments should be enough to have taught me this lesson!

The wise and perfect course is to think generous thoughts about others.

FRIDAY
WHATEVER IS NOBLE
Reading of the Day: II Samuel 9:1-11

David was not only "of nobility" as a king, but he also had noble thoughts. After all Saul had done to him, he sought out his only remaining descendant to show him kindness.

Memorize a portion of Philippians 4:8 by writing it out and placing it somewhere you will see it, repeating it to yourself several times throughout your day.

> "Finally, brothers, whatever is true,
> *whatever is noble…*
> think about such things."
> Philippians 4:8

The word *noble* is defined in the *American Heritage Dictionary* as "having or showing qualities of high moral character, as courage, generosity or honor."

Evaluate your thinking as you reflect on these questions:

- Are my thoughts of the highest moral character?

- Do they show courage and generosity?
- Do they demonstrate my position as a child of the King?

Focus today on noble thoughts, remembering King David's example.

SATURDAY
WHATEVER IS RIGHT
Reading of the Day: Daniel 3:16-28

Shadrach, Meshach, and Abednego knew the truth about false idols and the only true God. At great cost and with great courage, they chose to think on what was right and to do the right thing.

Add to your memory verse today the phrase "whatever is right."

> "Finally, brothers, whatever is true,
> whatever is noble, *whatever is right...*
> think about such things."
> Philippians 4:8

There is a difference between thinking on whatever is true and thinking on what is right. I have heard the saying, "Don't strive to do the next thing right, but do the next right thing." Think of an example in your life when you need a reminder to think and *do* what is right.

The questions to ask yourself today:

- Is my thinking and are my words right and appropriate?

- Are they in conformity with God's standards and principles?

- Do they build up others (and even myself) in a healthy way?

SUNDAY
WHATEVER IS PURE
Reading of the Day: Genesis 39:11-20

Joseph may not have confronted the "in your face" temptations today's technologically advanced society bombards us with. But to be sure, his temptations were alive, up front, and vividly technicolored!

Add another phrase today from Philippians 4:8:

"Finally, brothers, whatever is true,
whatever is noble, whatever is right,
whatever is pure...think about such things."

Ask yourself these questions, and "think on these things:"

- Are my motives pure?

- Are my thoughts and words holy?

- Am I living up to the standards and values I profess?

MONDAY
WHATEVER IS LOVELY
Reading of the Day: Luke 4:13-22

"All spoke well of him and were amazed at the gracious words that came from his lips. 'Isn't this Joseph's son?'" they asked.
Luke 4:22a

Keep memorizing!! I'm giving you plenty of days to work on this verse:

"Finally, brothers, whatever is true, whatever is noble, whatever is right, whatever is pure, *whatever is lovely…* think about such things."
Philippians 4:8

Jesus understood the thoughts and intentions of those around Him, yet He had compassion on sinners and spoke words which were lovely in the deepest sense of the word. The definition of "lovely" is "full of love, loving." That certainly describes our Savior and should describe us as well!

Ask yourself these questions:

- Do my thoughts and words have a beauty that appeals to the heart?

- Do they mirror the beauty and gentleness of Jesus?

TUESDAY
WHATEVER IS ADMIRABLE
Reading of the Day: Colossians 2:16-23

Whatever is aligned with the goodness of God is admirable. There are character traits I find admirable, such as patience and self-control. I also admire people with artistic talent, musicians that can play well, good conversationalists, and people with sharp memories, a good sense of humor or the ability to think fast on their feet.

Every man, whether a believer or not, has God-given talents and creativity. Sometimes people inadvertently glorify God through art or music or other means. All men are created by God and can reflect Him, whether they intend to or not. Spiritual qualities align with the goodness of God. As followers of Christ, we do well to reflect His character clearly through our natural abilities as well as our spiritual gifts.

Observe throughout your day "whatever is admirable."

WEDNESDAY
IF THERE IS ANY EXCELLENCE
Reading of the Day: Luke 10:38-42

"Mary has chosen what is better."
Luke 10:42b

Continue to memorize Philippians 4:8:

"Finally, brothers, whatever is true,
whatever is noble, whatever is right,
whatever is pure, whatever is lovely,
whatever is admirable—
if anything is excellent… think about such things."

Why shoot for Amazon, if you can have Amazon Prime? Why shoot for Kindle if you can have Kindle Fire? Why shoot for good if you can have excellent?

"And this is my prayer… that you may
be able to discern what is best."
Philippians 1:9a, 10a

Ask yourself these questions:

- Is what I am saying or doing of the highest quality?
- Is it just adequate or is it the best?

THURSDAY
ANYTHING WORTHY OF PRAISE
Reading of the Day: Acts 16:22-34

Add in the final phrase to memorize Philippians 4:8:

> "Finally, brothers, whatever is true,
> whatever is noble, whatever is right,
> whatever is pure, whatever is lovely,
> whatever is admirable,
> if anything is excellent or *praiseworthy*… think
> about such things."

On many days in recent years, I have found myself in distress. At times like that, it's very hard to fill my mind with things worthy of praise. Sometimes my praiseworthy thought consists in the cry, "Please, Lord! Give me relief just for one day!"

I am challenged by the example of Paul and Silas singing in the dungeon. (And they weren't singing the blues!) It often takes a conscious choice, but I (we) *can* think on things worthy of praise.

Ask yourself these questions today:

- Are my thoughts commendable?

- Am I focusing on thanking Him rather than the discomfort of my circumstances?

- Am I (and is God) proud of the way I am thinking and speaking?

FRIDAY
LET YOUR MIND DWELL
ON THESE THINGS!
Reading of the Day: Psalm 145:8-21

Take one more day to reflect on the entire verse of Philippians 4:8:

"Finally, brothers, whatever is true, whatever is
noble, whatever is right,
whatever is pure, whatever is lovely,
whatever is admirable
if anything is excellent or praiseworthy,
think about such things."

What you think must be true to what the Bible says—true according to God's character as revealed in His Word. As God uses His Word in your life and enables you to "think about such things," He will calm your fears about the future, the past, and the present. He will give you the energy and confidence necessary to deal with whatever you face in your life today.

SATURDAY
LIVING OUT THE VERBS
Reading of the Day: Philippians 4:9-13

The verse we've been memorizing, picking apart, and fleshing out for the past several days should teach us to meditate—to think and rethink on these things.

The verse that follows says,

> "Whatever you have *learned* or *received* or *heard* from me, or *seen* in me—put it into *practice*. And the God of peace *will be with* you."
> Philippians 4:9

Identify each of the verbs in the passage above. Pray that God would enable you to live out those verbs in your own life today.

Verse 11 of the same chapter says, "I have *learned* to be content in whatever circumstances I am."

Pray that God would give you a teachable heart as you meet each new circumstance that the day presents... learning, receiving, hearing, practicing... and experiencing His peace in the midst of it.

SUNDAY
ONE OF THOSE DAYS
Reading of the Day: Psalm 34:15-20

Do you ever have one of those days when your heart aches, your spirit flags, and you struggle to have a good attitude as you head into your day? I hope today is not one of those days for you! Let God's Word take priority over what you think, feel, and do today. Through His Word He will release His power in your life—power that allows you to think radically different thoughts which can change your life and your conduct. God's Word will draw you into a closer relationship with Him. As you walk closer to Him, you will also experience His power in your life.

"Hezekiah trusted in the LORD, the God of Israel. There was no one like him among all the kings of Judah, either before him or after him."
II Kings 18:5

"The righteous person may have many troubles, but the LORD delivers him from them all."
Psalm 34:19

MONDAY
EARTHQUAKE!
Reading of the Day: Psalm 46

Living in Costa Rica, we always had to be prepared for earthquakes. Though we went through a few quakes that were strong, the most serious damage we ever had were a few broken picture frames. But let me assure you, those earthquakes were scary enough!

When I read Psalm 46:1-2, I have just an inkling of the significance of the confidence David placed in His God.

"God is our refuge and strength,
an ever-present help in trouble.
Therefore we will not fear, though the earth give way
and the mountains fall into the heart of the sea."

Thank God right now that He is your ever-present help in trouble.

TUESDAY
SHIBBOLETH
Reading of the Day: I John 5:5-15

"Whoever has the Son has life; whoever does not have the Son of God does not have life."
I John 5:12

Many schools in Wisconsin and Illinois recognize Casimir Pulaski Day which honors a Polish Revolutionary War hero. Pulaski was so admired by General George Washington that his name was used as the password to identify friend or foe crossing battle lines. The name "Pulaski" could literally save your life!

It reminds me of the word *Shibboleth* in Judges 12. To identify fugitives, the men of Gilead would ask, 'Are you an Ephraimite?' If he said, 'No,' they then asked him to pronounce "Shibboleth." If anyone pronounced it "Sibboleth" instead, they would seize and kill him.

Just as that word was a test to see if a man belonged, today "Jesus Christ" is the password that saves our lives.

WEDNESDAY
LOOK TO THE HILLS!
Reading of the Day: Psalm 121

"I will lift up mine eyes unto the hills, from whence cometh my help."

I am pleased to include the following entry from my daughter, a, who works as a referral coordinator at a Christian clinic in Chicago which provides quality, affordable health care to the underserved communities on the West Side of Chicago. Here's what Kari wrote:

In Costa Rica, there was a hill with a well-worn path to the top where there was a cross that was visible from almost anywhere in the Central Valley. (Well, at least on the days when it wasn't shrouded in heavy mist and rain!) Any time that I felt alone or overwhelmed, I looked around me and found the cross; and the verses flitted through my mind, "I lift up my eyes to the hills."

Looking up at the mountains reminded me to lift my vision to something above my current circumstances, something far away from the stress and strain of the circumstances of life that were overwhelming me.

Even now in Illinois, where there is nothing that could even vaguely resemble a mountain, when I am consumed, I lift up my eyes to the sky (be it clear, rainy, or even snowy!) and remind myself that my help comes from the "maker of heaven and earth."

THURSDAY
SET YOUR HEART!
Reading of the Day: Psalm 27:4-8

"Who is he who will devote himself
to be close to me?"
Jeremiah 30:21b

Is the desire of your heart to experience a close, constant walk with God? If so, pray with me today,

I long more than anything else to know You.
I want You to be the center of my day-to-day life.
Prepare my heart to seek You today.

"[King Rehoboam] did evil because he had not set
his heart on seeking the Lord."
II Chronicles 12:14

Wouldn't it be great to please God today by setting your heart on seeking Him?

FRIDAY
WHAT'S HE UP TO?
Reading of the Day: Romans 12:1-8

I'd like to challenge you today to ask God what He is trying to do in your life—how He is trying to mold your character—

- People He longs for you to forgive

- Relationships He wants to heal

- Steps of obedience He wants you to take

Take a moment to think and pray about things God has brought to light through His Word, circumstances, conversations with others, and books you are reading. Make note of them, and begin to pray regularly that you might cooperate with the work of His Spirit as you are in process.

> "So here's what I want you to do,
> God helping you:
> Take your everyday, ordinary life—
> your sleeping, eating, going-to-work,
> and walking-around life—
> and place it before God as an offering.
> Embracing what God does for you is the best
> thing you can do for him."
> Romans 12:1 The Message

SATURDAY
THE TIME HAS COME
Reading of the Day: John 19:35-36; 20:24-31

> "Then Jesus told him, 'Because you
> have seen me, you have believed;
> blessed are those who have not seen
> and yet have believed.'"
> John 20:29

When we choose not to believe in God's love for us, He grieves as a heartbroken father. What more could God have done for you? What more do you wish He would say?

God understands it isn't easy to trust in a hand you

cannot see. You bring joy to His Father-heart when you step out in faith and believe, even when you do not feel; know. even when you cannot see. God gave His one and only Son to demonstrate His love.

Remember this phrase throughout your day:

The time has come to believe!

SUNDAY
ACQUIESCENCE VS. ACCEPTANCE
Reading of the Day: Ephesians 3:14-21

If I had one more day to write about a spiritual Lent, I would say to fast from acquiescence and feast on acceptance. There is a big difference between the two. I can either give up and resign myself to circumstances, *or* by faith I can accept what life deals me as something lovingly allowed by God's hand. Here is today's prayer of acceptance:

May I be content with any bed of Thy making. May I have a sense of wonder and vision to see what You are up to. You are an awesome Creator. Nothing is impossible for You. Out of my brokenness, You can forgive, cleanse, and start over, transplanting a pure heart in me and pulling me from the gravity of sin. Help me soar like an eagle in victory, ongoing obedience, steadfast spirit, and fruitful ministry.

"Now to him who is able to do immeasurably
more than all we ask or imagine,
according to his power that is at work within us."
Ephesians 3:20

MONDAY
CRYING OUT TO GOD
Reading: Psalm 55:1-8, 16-17, 22-23

Do you happen to have any problems today?
Declare aloud: (if you can)

"Evening, morning, and noon I cry to You!"

List a few of the challenges you face today, and then
meditate on these excerpts from Psalm 55.

My thoughts trouble me, and I am distraught. (v. 2b)
My heart is in anguish within me; (4a)
Fear and trembling have beset me; (5a)
But I call to God, and the LORD saves me. (16)
Evening, morning, and noon I cry out ...and he
hears my voice. (17)
Cast your cares on the LORD, and he will sustain
you; (22a)

Put your list of problems in His hands and declare:

"But as for me, I trust in you." (23b)

TUESDAY
HELEN'S LIST
Reading of the Day: Psalm 119:9-16

Don't you just love how voice-to-text sometimes interprets things? I "wrote out" a Puritan prayer the other day, saying "May holiness be the atmosphere in which I live." Siri interpreted this, saying, "May Helen's list be the atmosphere in which I live." I'm not sure what's on Helen's list today. I do know that Siri isn't the only one that has a hard time interpreting "HOLINESS."

Sin is a deadly malignancy in our lives, and sometimes we dig our claws into it, refusing to let go. We hold "polluting dalliance" with it, as the Puritan author would say. The dictionary defines dalliance as a brief or casual involvement. It's easy to take sin casually, briefly toying with the idea; taking lightly the consequences of words and actions.

I know something to add to Helen's list today:

Lord, may I refuse to hold polluting dalliance with sin today.

WEDNESDAY
RUN TO THE FATHER'S ARMS
Reading of the Day: Mark 10:13-16

When working at a community clinic, I used to give vaccinations to children. Parents were often upset at the thought of the pain their child was about to experience. Yet they knew it was necessary. Though the mom would hold her son tight so he could not escape the needle, she was still the one he would turn to for comfort.

The child's way is the only way to peace. The loving child trusts. We who know our God and have proved Him good in the past, also know that there we will find rest. Our Father does not always explain. *Somehow*, at *some* time the wrong will be made right. There is only one place to find peace—at the foot of the cross.

Run to the One you trust.

"If you, then, though you are evil, know how to
give good gifts to your children,
how much more will your Father in heaven give
good gifts to those who ask him!"
Matthew 7:11

THURSDAY
HE WILL CARRY YOU
Reading of the Day: Deuteronomy 1:26-31

While living in Bolivia, we had the privilege of ministering with our good friends, the Confers. The four of us sang a wonderful song together which talked about God's power to go beyond our biggest problems, our tallest mountain, our darkest storm and our deepest troubles. We sometimes feel we have the weight of the world on our shoulders. Jesus *did* carry the weight of the world on His shoulders.

Deuteronomy 1:31 paints a beautiful word picture of this concept. Moses is giving his farewell speech to the people of Israel when he says, "[In the wilderness] you saw how the Lord your God carried you, as a father carries his son." God does not just carry the weight of the world on His shoulders, he carries *you and me* as a father carries his son.

Take a moment to consider the burdens you are carrying today. Now, lay those at Jesus' feet and let Him pick you up and carry you through the difficult spots on the path of life.

FRIDAY
BLESSING OF THE DAY
Reading of the Day: Psalm 63:1-8

Over the next several days, I want to share one blessing a day, based on my prayers for my children and grandchildren. I want to leave a rich spiritual heritage for them and let you share in that experience.

Today my blessing for you is that
God would grant you a
JOYFUL, DYNAMIC FAITH

I challenge you today to love God, and *love loving* God! Let Him be the joy of your life. Share that joy and passion with others. Don't let emotions and the circumstances of life make your joy falter. Pray today,

Let me thirst for You! Help me long to love You more!

Only through the Spirit's help can your faith become more joyful and dynamic.

"O God, you are my God, earnestly I seek you...
Because your love is better than life,
my lips will glorify you."
Psalm 63:1, 3

SATURDAY
BLESSING OF THE DAY
Reading of the Day: I Thessalonians 2:10-13

MAY GOD BLESS YOU WITH A RICH AND INTIMATE PRAYER LIFE AND PROFOUND JOY IN HIS WORD

May you hunger and thirst for Him, claim His promises, find comfort in His kindness, share your heart with Him, and listen to Him—taking moments of silence and meditating on God's Word. May you follow Christ's example of having the Word be part of your daily vocabulary and feel at ease sharing it with others. May you take Scripture and appropriate it in prayer.

The only way to fail in prayer is to not show up.
—Thomas Keating

"And now we look back on all this and thank God,
an artesian well of thanks!
When you got the Message of God we preached,
you didn't pass it off as just one
more human opinion,
but you took it to heart as God's true
word to you, which it is,
God himself at work in you believers!"
I Thessalonians 2:13 The Message

SUNDAY
BLESSING OF THE DAY
**Reading of the Day: Reflect on
your identity in the following verses:
John 15:15, Ephesians 2:10, Colossians 2:10**

MAY YOU EXPERIENCE WHOLENESS AND SECURITY IN CHRIST

Today's world pounds insecurity into our lives. When Woody bought me Beth Moore's book, *So Long, Insecurity: You've Been a Bad Friend to Us,* it took me a long time to pick it up and read it. The close-up picture of the author's face on the cover looked *too* perfect. Though I know that Moore has dealt with her own insecurities, my mind just couldn't stop thinking, "If I looked *that* good, maybe it would be *easy* to say good-bye to insecurity!"

I often need to remind myself that our wholeness and security are found in Christ and the truths of God's Word. Among those truths: I am His friend (John 15:15) and His workmanship (Eph. 2:10). Think on other Scriptures that declare who you are in Him, and note them somewhere to remind you to meditate on them throughout your day.

"And in Him you have been made complete."
Colossians 2:10a NASB

MONDAY
BLESSING OF THE DAY
Reading of the Day: John 14:25-31; 16:32, 33

MAY YOU KNOW AND EXPERIENCE
GOD'S PEACE

The Tibas River ran near us in Costa Rica. I would often take my prayer walk, crossing a bridge over the Tibas.

Knowing God's peace is not the same as a still pond, reflecting the landscape around it. I had to be talked into my one and only experience with whitewater rafting on the Sarapiqui. (I call it "white-knuckle rafting!") As I recall, there was only one short segment that was straight and calm. The rest of the time was full of difficult and dangerous turns, ranging from Class I to Class IV.

Life is a bit like a river that has short, peaceful segments, but otherwise is full of unexpected turns and rough waters that are difficult to navigate.

Note in today's Scripture reading we are promised grief and troubles as well as peace. May you know and experience God's peace in life's Class IV rapids!

"For this is what the LORD says: 'I will extend
peace to her like a river.'"
Isaiah 66:12

TUESDAY
BLESSING OF THE DAY:
PEACE PART II
Reading of the Day: Isaiah 48:12-19

Yesterday's blessing merits another day's contemplation.

MAY YOU KNOW AND EXPERIENCE
GOD'S PEACE

"If only you had paid attention to my commands,
your peace would have been like a river, your righteousness like the waves of the sea." Isaiah 48:18

I would love to have my peace be like a river, my
righteousness like the waves of the sea! A river is fed
by springs, an ongoing source of fresh water. Are
you drinking daily from the fresh water of God's
Word?

A river ends in a body of water. **Your present life
is not your destination**. Live today with an awareness of your need to stay connected to the Source,
and remember your destination is a heavenly one!

WEDNESDAY
BLESSING OF THE DAY
Reading of the Day: I John 2:9-11; 3:14-16

MAY YOU LOVE ALL PEOPLE OF THE WORLD WITHOUT EXCEPTION

Growing up in Minnesota in the 50's and 60's, I had little exposure to people of other races and cultures. I thank God I was not only taught respect for all people, but also was encouraged to learn about others through books and our faithful *World Book Encyclopedia*. When I was privileged as a teen to travel to Mexico to teach vacation Bible school in a rural area, I fell in love with the Mexican children. Suddenly the words to the song, "Jesus Loves the Little Children," took on a real face of color:

> *Red and yellow, black and white,*
> *they are precious in His sight.*

"But anyone who hates a brother or sister is in the darkness and walks around in the darkness. They do not know where they are going, because the darkness has blinded them."
I John 2:11

THURSDAY
BLESSING OF THE DAY
Reading of the Day: I John 2:28 – 3:3

MAY YOU REFLECT THE CHARACTER
AND PRIORITIES OF CHRIST

I cannot think of a simpler, more inspirational (**and** challenging) life goal than to reflect the character and priorities of our Lord Jesus.

As you read God's Word, observe what priorities and character traits are pleasing to God. For instance, Jesus obviously dedicated time and effort to the study of the Scriptures. He read, meditated, memorized, and applied them to Himself and others.

List three character traits or priorities of Christ you should be reflecting. Pray specifically that God would be forming and transforming you today in those areas.

"But grow in the grace and knowledge of our Lord
and Savior Jesus Christ."
II Peter 3:18

FRIDAY
BLESSING OF THE DAY
Reading of the Day: Luke 9:23-27

MAY YOU BE A DISCIPLE WHO MAKES DISCIPLES

Strive to be an authentic disciple who is learning and applying biblical truth 24/7. God is looking for men and women who live all-out for Him. Pray each day you might serve Him heartily in whatever you are doing, whether teaching from God's Word or brushing your teeth. Spend time with Him, so people around you see JESUS in your words, attitudes, and actions. As you interact with others, share God's faithfulness with them. Tell them what you are learning from Him. Discipleship is all about being all about HIM!

"And whatever you do, whether in word or deed, do it all in the name of the Lord Jesus."
Colossians 3:17a

SATURDAY
BLESSING OF THE DAY
Reading of the Day: Mark 3:20, 21, 31-35

MAY YOU SERVE GOD FERVENTLY

The current American Christian culture puts a heavy emphasis on margin, rest, and taking care of your personal needs. There is a clear need for margin and rest, but Jesus also set an example of sacrifice that we should not forget as we serve God.

> *Once we adopt a heart of sacrifice, that we*
> *are here to serve at God's good pleasure,*
> *everything else tends to fall into place.*
> —Gary Thomas

Self-obsession can become a character cancer. It's easy to have "margin" turn into an excuse for self-service at the expense of sacrificial service.

One way to reflect the character and priorities of Christ is to **serve God fervently.**

> "My Father is always at his work to this very day,
> and I too am working."
> John 5:16

SUNDAY
LIVE YOUR DAY
Reading of the Day: Matthew 25:31-40

> *How we live our days is how we live our lives.*
> —Anne Dillard

If you are wondering what God wants you to do with your life, focus on today. You need to discover how to live one day at a time in faithful surrender to

God, as you "continue to work out your salvation with fear and trembling." Philippians 2:12

As you make daily decisions and prioritize your life, ask yourself the question, "Is this the most loving way I can live my life? Am I loving my God and my neighbor by living the way I live, driving how I drive, or talking how I talk?" As you come into contact with people today, live as though each of those individuals were Christ Himself.

"For 'whatever you do to the least of these, you do also to Me.'" Matthew 25:40

MONDAY
STAND OR FLEE?
Reading of the Day: Look up References Below

John Bunyan's refusal to stop preaching kept him in prison for twelve years. He shared biblical insights about whether to stand or flee in the face of suffering. He wrote, "Thou mayest do in this as it is in thy heart. If it is in thy heart to fly, fly: if it be in thy heart to stand, stand. The same man may both fly and stand, as the call and working of God with his heart may be."

Moses fled. Exodus 2:15	Moses stood. Hebrews 11:27
David fled. I Samuel 19:12	David stood. I Samuel 24:8
Jeremiah fled. Jeremiah 37:11-12	Jeremiah stood. Jeremiah 38:17
Christ withdrew. Luke 9:10	Christ stood. John 18:1-8
Paul fled. 2 Cor. 11:33	Paul stood. Acts 20:22-23

Honor God today, whether you are called to stand or called to flee.

TUESDAY
JOY-STEALERS AND BAR-BREAKERS
Reading of the Day: Romans 8:1-4

"I broke the bars of your yoke and enabled you to walk with heads held high."
Leviticus 26:13

There are joy-stealers right and left in this life. I can think of more than one in my own life right now! How do we get past the joy-stealers and let God break the bars of our yoke, allowing us to walk with heads held high?

Set your mind today on the things of the Spirit, for

that produces life and peace. "The law of the Spirit of life in Christ Jesus has set you free from the law of sin and death." (Romans 8:2)

Pray with me today:

Lord, break the bars of my joy-stealers today!
Give me the discipline to look on the things of the Spirit,
So that I may be a living example of life and peace.

WEDNESDAY
GOD'S DEFINITION OF RIGHTEOUS
Reading of the Day: Psalm 5

"For surely, O Lord, You bless the righteous;
You surround them with Your favor as with a shield."
Psalm 5:12

If I were to suggest adjectives to describe myself, I seriously doubt "righteous" would be among them. In fact, it's hard for me to get my brain around the concept of the word, let alone *be* that! But the psalmist tells us to cry out to God in expectation. Only through Him, can we confidently count ourselves among the righteous surrounded with His favor.

Pray this prayer with me today:

O, Father, please help me to be Your idea of righteous.
I know that on my own, my righteousness
is as filthy rags before You.
But I have invited Jesus to be my Savior and Lord,
and I long to daily walk with You.
Help me to be a living example of His righteousness!

THURSDAY
PRECIOUS IN HIS SIGHT
Reading of the Day: Isaiah 43:1-4

I believe God's feelings towards you are consistent with His feelings towards the people of Israel. I believe that He will hear you and bless you, as you pray these words over your own life and the lives of your loved ones today.

"Don't be afraid, I've redeemed you.
I've called your name. You're mine.
When you're in over your head, I'll be there with you.
When you're in rough waters, you will not go down.
When you're between a rock and a hard place,
it won't be a dead end—
Because I am God, your personal God,
The Holy of Israel, your Savior."
Portions of Isaiah 43:1-4 taken from The Message

If God so leads you, call a loved one and pray for them, based on the above passage.

FRIDAY
RESPOND IN PRAISE
Reading of the Day: Psalm 34:1-10

"I will extol the LORD at all times;
his praise will always be on my lips."
Psalm 34:1

Even the best of us get discouraged. Billy Graham wrote, "The Christian life is not a constant high. I have my moments of deep discouragement." When facing times of discouragement, the psalmist's advice still holds. After all, he writes *all* times and *always*. Praising Him may not change your circumstances, but it will change your heart attitude and at the same time bring glory to God.

During your day, you are sure to face something discouraging. Make a pact right now with God,

*"When I'm tempted to be discouraged today,
I will praise You!"*

PS Dear Lord, help me **remember** this pact with you and *keep* it!

SATURDAY
CONSULT GOD FIRST
Reading of the Day: Joshua 9:14-21

I have to laugh when one of our daughters is watching a movie she has seen time and time again. When the protagonists are about to make a wrong choice, she coaches them aloud, "No, don't do it!"

That was my exact response when I recently read Joshua chapters 7-9. Here the Israelites made their first big errors upon entering the Promised Land. After Moses' interminable farewell address, you'd think they would recall ***consulting God first***.

Not!

After Jericho, they confidently sent up just a few thousand men to take Ai. Humbled by their rout, God sent them back to victory with 30,000 troops. Then they made a treaty with the men of Gibeon, "and did not ask for the counsel of the Lord." (Joshua 9:14) That mistake would prove to be a thorn in their flesh for years to come.

How often do we make the same mistakes?!?

Consult Him first!

SUNDAY
MISTY WEATHER
Reading of the Day: Psalm 6:1-4

"Lord, my God, may Your unfailing
love be my comfort,
According to Your promise to Your servant!"
Psalm 119:76

Should misty weather try
The temper of the soul,
Come, Lord, and purge and fortify
And let Thy hands make whole.
—Amy Carmichael

Where do you turn for comfort when the going gets tough? Make it your habit to immediately run to His unfailing love and promises.

"May Your unfailing love be my comfort!"

Make this your breath prayer today. Write it down somewhere you will see it frequently during your day and recall it often.

SATURDAY
IN GOOD COMPANY
Reading of the Day: Romans 7:14-20

I fall into the same traps over and over again. I have character flaws. I fail. I am pitifully aware of my weaknesses and shortcomings. And, yes, I even sin. But I'm in good company!

> "I do not understand what I do.
> For what I want to do I do not do,
> but what I hate I do."
> Paul in Romans 7:15

When we *do* sin, let us see it not only as an opportunity to repent and seek God's forgiveness, but also to experience a teaching moment. We may as well learn a lesson from it!

> *Genuine repentance renews the soul*
> *like few other activities*
> *and places us in a posture of learning.*
> —Gary Thomas

As the classic Christian writer, Fenelon, put it, "These imperfections which remain in good souls serve to humble them, to detach them from themselves, to make them feel their own weakness, to make them run more eagerly to thee."

May your imperfections make you run eagerly to Him today.

SUNDAY
SPANISH PHRASE OF THE DAY
Reading of the Day: Mark 10:35-45

PARA SERVIRLE

"For even the Son of Man did not come to be
served, but to serve."
Mark 10:45a

In Costa Rica they don't use the most common
Spanish phrase for "you're welcome." Instead, Ticos
will reply, "Para servirle." Literally that means, "I'm
at your service." Technically, it could also mean,
"I'm here to serve him." I sort of like that last twist
on this phrase, which can easily become a mindless
response.

Think about the English phrase, "You're welcome."
What does that mean? Welcome to what? I think it
means that most gladly you have done something
from your heart. But I doubt you've ever given that
phrase much consideration.

Remember you are on this earth...

PARA SERVIRLE.

MONDAY
BIG POWER!
Reading of the Day: Ephesians 1:18-23

BIG POWER CAN ACCOMPLISH *little things!*

Resurrection power! The last portion of Ephesians 1 includes phrases like "surpassing power" and "the working of the strength of His might which He brought about in Christ, when He raised Him from the dead." (Ephesians 1:19, 20) A power like that can accomplish BIG THINGS!

But what about the little things, like what is on my mind right now? As I write this, I'm struggling to let go of a small, unintentional slight by a friend. The little things are sometimes more difficult to budge than the **MOUNTAINS!**

Lord, if you could raise Jesus from the dead
by Your awesome power,
surely I can trust You to blast away the little,
stubborn spots in my heart!

TUESDAY
ETERNAL ENCOURAGEMENT
Reading of the Day: II Thessalonians 2:13-17

There are few blessings I enjoy more than II Thessalonians 2:16-17

"May our Lord Jesus Christ himself
and God our Father,
who loved us and by his grace gave us eternal
encouragement and good hope,
encourage your hearts and strengthen
you in every good deed and word."

How amazing to be plugged in to the source of *eternal* encouragement! Unlike the world, we have reason for *good hope*, true hope. The all-powerful God Himself encourages you and strengthens you, producing an inner strength that leads to both action and speech.

Take a moment to turn to God, using this passage as the framework for your prayer.

WEDNESDAY
FILL YOUR NAME IN THE BLANK!
Reading of the Day: I Peter 1:1-5

"To God's chosen people who are temporary
residents [in the world] and are
scattered throughout the provinces of Pontus,
Galatia, Cappadocia, Asia, and Bithynia.
God the Father knew you long ago and chose you
to live holy lives with the Spirit's help."
I Peter 1:1 God's Word

Peter was writing this letter to a specific group of Christ-followers, but they were spread out in many provinces. Peter's words can be easily applied to all those who have been marked by God, whatever state, country, or province you find yourself in.

Take a moment to personalize the above passage by filling your name in the blank. For example, substitute your name for "God's chosen people" and your city, state, country, and global region in place of the areas mentioned.

Here is my prayer for you today:

To _____, chosen by God, made holy
by God's Holy Spirit,
a stranger and alien in the world who has been
cleansed by the blood of Jesus Christ.
May God show you good will and
fill your life with peace.

THURSDAY
SURROUNDED!
Reading of the Day: Psalm 91:1-10

Dr. and Mrs. Nelson Bell served as missionaries in China from 1916 to 1941. During a time of military unrest, they lay in their dugout shelter, unsure of their future. Mrs. Bell wrote, "We were counting our defenses…"

- Overhead are the overshadowing wings. (Ps 91:4)

- Underneath are the everlasting arms. (Deut 33:27)

- All around "the angel of the Lord encampteth round about them that fear Him, and delivereth them." (Ps 34:7)

- Inside, the 'Peace which passeth all understanding,' (Phil 4:7) and "Thou wilt keep him in perfect peace, whose mind is stayed on Thee." (Is 26:3)

Review your defenses today, and remind yourself, "I am surrounded!"

*Scripture references from KJV

FRIDAY
VICE AND VIRTUE
Reading of the Day: II Peter 1:3-9

"For if you possess these qualities in increasing measure, they will keep you from being ineffective and unproductive in your knowledge of our Lord Jesus Christ."
II Peter 1:8

Francis De Sales wrote about temptation, "Treat the vice with the opposite virtue."

I find that to be an interesting concept. If your weakness is gossip, make a consistent effort to note positive qualities in others and praise them. If anxiety, find things to be thankful for. If gluttony, give your cookies away (advice I should have followed before polishing off that last package of Oreos!)

What is your vice? What is the opposite virtue? Try out DeSales' recommendation today.

> *Just as failing in one area slowly eats*
> *away at our spiritual lives,*
> *so improving in one area, even a small one,*
> *nourishes our spiritual lives.*
> —Gary Thomas

SATURDAY
HONEST DOUBTS
Reading of the Day: Judges 6:11-24

God does put up with honest doubts. Take Gideon, for example. Though we clearly see his doubts, Gideon also had a certain level of trust and hope in God. The angel of the Lord first appeared to Gideon, saying, "The Lord is with you, O valiant warrior."

Gideon's reply implies he'd spent time trying to figure out what God was doing. "O my lord, if the Lord is with us, why then has all this happened to us?" Once again the angel confirmed God's call.

"Go in this your strength and deliver Israel… Have I not sent you?"

Gideon argued that he was a nobody. This time the angel replied, "Surely I will be with you."

The story goes on and on with Gideon's doubts. In turn, God responded with plenty of evidence and lots of encouragement to grow his faith. All God asked in return was Gideon's cooperation.

> *Doubts are the ants in the pants of faith;*
> *They keep it awake and moving.*
> —Frederich Buechner

SUNDAY
GOOD EXAMPLE, BAD EXAMPLE
Reading of the Day: Judges 7:9-18

There is much to learn from both the good and the bad examples in the Bible. Think with me again today about Gideon. (Judges 6-8) Gideon was a man of valor, but he was willing to admit his own fears. The Lord said to him, "But if you are afraid to attack, go down to the camp with Purah your servant." He went with Purah—*an **honest admission of fear!***

When he heard the Midianites interpret a dream about Israel's victory, "*He bowed in worship.*" **Great response!**

When he called the attack, he had the men cry, "For the Lord and for Gideon!" ***Right priorities!***

When the men asked him to rule over them, he replied, "I will not… the *Lord shall rule over you.*" ***Way to go, Gideon!***

Then he asked the men for gold to make an ephod to "play the harlot." ***Bad, Gideon!***

Imitate the good example. Learn from the bad.

MONDAY
THE GOOD SHEPHERD
Reading of the Day: Ezekiel 34:11-16

"The Lord is my Shepherd; I shall not be in want."
Psalm 23:1

Some Bible passages are so familiar that their impact is diminished. Ezekiel chapter 34 actually brings new life to Psalm 23. First, God reprimands the shepherds of Israel for not strengthening the sickly, healing the diseased, binding up the broken, or bringing back the scattered. In contrast, He tells His people, "Behold, I Myself will search for My sheep and seek them out… I will care for My sheep and will deliver them… I will feed them on the mountains… They will lie down on good grazing ground… I will seek the lost, bring back the scattered, bind up the broken, and strengthen the sick."

What can the Good Shepherd do for you today?

TUESDAY
MAKING GOD RECOGNIZABLE
Reading of the Day: I Peter 4:7-11

"Whatever you do, do all to the glory of God."
I Corinthians 10:31

We have been created for the glory of God. That is a hard concept for me to get my mind around. The Greek word for glory is *doxa,* which means "the true apprehension of God... His unchanging essence... ascribing to Him His full recognition." God wants to make Himself recognizable **to** us and **through** us. Living a life that glorifies God is synonymous with living a life that reveals God. As imperfect as we are, we can still be used to make God recognizable through our lives. As we grow in spiritual maturity, the Spirit of Christ becomes more recognizable in us.

Lord, help people to catch a glimpse of
Your invisible character through me.

WEDNESDAY
ALL HE ASKS IS OBEDIENCE
Reading of the Day: Exodus 19:4-8

"Now if you obey me fully and keep my covenant,
then out of all nations you will be
my treasured possession."
Exodus 19:5

In the passage above, God asks the simplest (yet at
the same time most difficult) thing He could require of us. The best way to "fully obey" is to obey
right now in the smallest thing that you are facing.
Maybe one of the following would be a challenge
from God for you right now:

Will you choose not to talk about those who
treat you wrongly?

Will you walk away from that movie or turn off
that TV program?

Will you put down your book for a minute and
look at mine?

Will you stop complaining, and give thanks
instead?

Will you take a moment to speak to someone
who is hurting?

Will you throw yourself into My loving arms
and cry, "Not my will, but YOURS!"

Will you listen to Me tell you, "Be still and know that I am God"? (Psalm 46:10)

Will you choose to think on what is good, honorable, and right?

Take a moment to think about what small ways God might be asking you to be obedient.

THURSDAY
NONE OF IT!
Reading of the Day: Isaiah 30:15-21

"This is what the Sovereign LORD,
the Holy One of Israel, says:
'In repentance and rest is your salvation,
In quietness and trust is your strength,'
But you would have none of it."
Isaiah 30:15

We often quote the first part of Isaiah 30:15. The tragedy lies in the last part of the verse. Though God promised salvation and strength, they would have none of it!

We are often guilty of the same. We struggle and fret and worry. We don't like living with anxiety and weakness, but we forget to put into practice God's formula for salvation and strength. They come through repentance and rest, through quietness and trust.

Claim the promises of Isaiah 30:15.

Lord, I believe my strength comes
through complete dependence on You,
turning back to You in quiet confidence. Amen.

FRIDAY
LONGING TO BE HOLY
Reading of the Day: Romans 7:21-8:4

"I am the LORD your God;
Consecrate yourselves and be holy,
because I am holy."
Leviticus 11:44a

Striving, failing, striving, failing. That is the cycle I think of when I think of my own struggle to attain personal holiness. If I direct all my efforts toward *not* disobeying, I enter into a vicious cycle of frustration.

But if the burden of striving is replaced with a longing to know God in an ever more intimate way, slowly, surely, holiness will be the result.

Lord, help me to rest in You today.
May I apply myself today to do nothing and think
nothing which may displease You.
While I simply strive to know
You in an ever more intimate way,
I rest and trust in You to make me holy like You.

SATURDAY
ROCK, SNUGGLE AND SING
Reading of the Day: Zephaniah 3:14-20

"The LORD your God is with you,
he is mighty to save.
He will take great delight in you,
he will quiet you with his love,
he will rejoice over you with singing."
Zephaniah 3:17

I've had the privilege of being with each of my grandchildren shortly after they were born, and counted it all joy to do my best to comfort them when crying—rocking, snuggling, and singing over them. I take great delight in my grandkids, just as I did in my own children. Take that visual image today, and put yourself in God's arms. No matter whether you are smiling or crying, He takes great delight in you, quieting you with His love, rejoicing over you with singing!

SUNDAY
AN EXTRAORDINARY SPIRIT
Reading of the Day: Daniel 5:5-12

There are several amazing stories in the book of Daniel. I am struck by the queen's description after the handwriting on the wall:

> "The king's face grew pale and his thoughts
> alarmed him, and his hip joints went slack
> and his knees began knocking together."
> Daniel 5:6 NASB

(Don't you just love that description?!? Have you ever felt that way?)

The queen coolly approached the king to tell him of an 80-year-old man who had "an ***extraordinary spirit***, knowledge and insight," (probably even able to quickly solve expert level Sudoku puzzles!)

Caleb was also described as having a "***different spirit.***" (Numbers 14) As we live in our overindulged, self-absorbed culture, let's hope God the Father occasionally nudges His Son, and says of you or me, "Hey! Doesn't *she* have an extraordinary spirit? Doesn't *he* stick out?"

MONDAY
TO INQUIRE OR NOT TO INQUIRE
Reading of the Day: Judges 19:19-30
(Parental Guidance Suggested!)

At the end of the period of the judges of Israel, the people inconsistently sought the Lord's counsel. The book of Judges tells the horrific story about the concubine who was ravished and killed and then cut into pieces to send to all the tribes. It's interesting to read the passage and note how many times people use words such as "vile" and "disgraceful" to describe others. Yet who was *most* wrong, *most* responsible? Did *anyone* consistently seek God's counsel or help?

The Levite and his host offered the Levite's concubine to the "worthless fellows" in the city. They didn't turn to God for a better suggestion! *Finally*, the Israelites all asked His counsel as they prepared for civil war. Later, in chapter 21, after the loss of thousands of soldiers but eventual victory with God's help, they once again had forgotten to inquire of the Lord when they made critical plans. It's no wonder the final verse of Judges characterizes this time by saying,

> "In those days Israel had no king,
> everyone did as he saw fit."
> Judges 21:25

Remember today…

INQUIRE CONSISTENTLY!
Seek what is right in God's eyes.

TUESDAY
AN OLD-FASHIONED VALUE
Reading of the Day: Ephesians 1:4-9

God is love. We often hear that phrase.

But how often do you hear **God is kind?** God's kindness is mentioned again and again in His Word!

Look at these phrases:

- But with <u>everlasting kindness</u> I will have mercy on you. Isaiah 54:8

- According to the <u>kind intention</u> of His will. Ephesians 1:5

- According to His <u>kind intention</u> which He purposed in Him. Ephesians 1:9

- Consider therefore the <u>kindness</u> ... of God ... <u>kindness</u> to you, provided that you continue in his <u>kindness</u>. Romans 11:22

Be kind today! Make this your prayer:

Lord, I long to reflect Your character today.
Help me to be kind, even as I continue in Your kindness.

WEDNESDAY
ANOTHER OLD-FASHIONED VALUE: GENTLENESS
Reading of the Day: Titus 3:1-8

"Remind the people... to be peaceable and considerate, and always to be gentle toward everyone." Titus 3:1-2

As a nurse, I have felt that gentleness should be a characteristic of all medical professionals. I would imagine you can think of some nurses or doctors who have been gentle. Then, on the other hand…

How often have you prayed that God would help you be gentle? Gentleness is promised us as a fruit of the spirit, but it doesn't usually come easily. We must nourish the fruit of gentleness in our thoughts, or it will not be evidenced in our behavior. Often God allows us to go through suffering to develop in us a spirit of gentleness.

Without the scars of Calvary in our lives, we will not exhibit "the soft, sweet, gentle, restful, victorious, overflowing and triumphant life that flows like a spring morning from an empty tomb."
—G.D.W.

> *I choose gentleness… Nothing is won by force.*
> *I choose to be gentle. If I raise my voice,*
> *may it be only in praise.*
> *If I clench my fist, may it be only in prayer.*
> *If I make a demand, may it be only of myself.*
> —Max Lucado

THURSDAY
CHOOSE CONTENTMENT
Reading of the Day: Hebrews 13:5-9

I know that I've written about contentment already on other days of the calendar, but the subject bears repeating. Whenever we think we've risen up to the challenge of being content, we realize a truth that Thomas à Kempis wrote of, "I often boast to myself of the gift of contentment—as long as everything goes according to my wishes and views."

What is your contentment based on today? When things don't go according to your wishes and views, choose contentment anyway.

> "Keep your lives free from the love of money and
> be content with what you have."
> Hebrews 13:5a

FRIDAY
GO IN THE STRENGTH OF THE
LORD GOD!
Reading of the Day: Psalm 71:12-21

I ask you to meditate today on one phrase. First, notice it in context in the reading in Psalm 71.

> "But I will hope continually
> And will praise You yet more and more.

My mouth shall tell of Your righteousness
And Your salvation all the day,
For I do not know their limits.
I will go in the strength of the Lord GOD;
I will make mention of Your righteousness, of
Yours only."
Psalm 71:14-16 NKJV

Say this (aloud, if possible) at least five times. Write it down to look at it often and commit it to memory. And meditate on this incredible phrase throughout your day:

I will go in the strength of the Lord God!

SATURDAY
OH, HOW HE LOVES YOU AND ME!
Reading of the Day: I John 4:13-21

"The disciple whom <u>Jesus loved</u>…"
John 21:7a

Did you ever notice it doesn't say, "The follower who <u>loved Jesus</u>?" If we want to see the perfect model of love, let's focus on *His* love for *us*, not *our* love for *Him*.

Once in a church service, the congregation was singing, "Oh, how I love You!" After hearing that phrase sung over and over again, I turned to Woody and whispered, "I think He knows how much I love Him, and that embarrasses me a bit. I don't think I'll boast of it."

God is the one who gives us both the *will* and the *ability* to love Him.

> "First we were loved, now we love.
> He loved us first."
> I John 4:19 The Message

Instead of the chorus repeating how much we love God, let's sing today,

> *Oh, how He loves you and me!*

SUNDAY
PLEASE COOPERATE!
Reading of the Day: II Corinthians 1:8-11

> "Please cooperate, (in prayer for us)
> so that God will continue to preserve us
> as we trust in Him, and as you faithfully pray."
> II Corinthians 1:11 *(Su's paraphrase)*

I ask you to take one day to pray specifically for us and our ministry as we continue to serve God with the desire to *live* as authentic disciples of the Lord Jesus and to *make* disciples. Pray that God gives us grace and wisdom as we invest in the lives of others in our community and around the world.

One of the theme verses of our ministry is
II Timothy 2:2:
"And the things you have heard me say in the
presence of many witnesses
entrust to reliable people who will also be qualified
to teach others."

MONDAY
WHERE WOULD I BE?
Reading of the Day: Isaiah 38:13-17

Junior high years can be rough. We all know that. During my own junior high years, I passed through moments of despair. I longed to know God more and strove to spend more time in God's Word, but life was one huge struggle. It was during those years I memorized the following verse:

"Lo, for my own welfare I had great bitterness;
It is You who has kept my soul from
the pit of nothingness,
For You have cast all my sins behind Your back."
Isaiah 38:17 NASB

Truly, without God, where would we be? I cannot thank Him enough for His mercy demonstrated in my own life! What about you?

TUESDAY
EAVESDROPPING ON HANNAH
Reading of the Day: I Samuel 1:9-18

Dedicated to my granddaughter Hannah

The Bible gives us remarkable stories of women of faith. How precious that God gives us an intimate glimpse into Hannah's heart! In the book of I Samuel, we are led quietly to the bench right next to Hannah as she pours out her heart before God. Eli the priest sees her lips moving and thinks she is drunk. But God allows us to hear her whispered prayer.

> "And she made a vow, saying,
> 'Lord Almighty, if you will only look on
> your servant's misery
> and remember me, and not forget your
> servant but give her a son,
> then I will give him to the Lord for
> all the days of his life.'"
> I Samuel 1:11a

Hannah told Eli she was not drunk but was pouring out her soul before the Lord. Take a moment to call on the Lord of hosts, and sincerely pour your heart out before Him.

WEDNESDAY
SHORT VERSE; LONG CHAPTER
Reading of the Day: Psalm 119:89-96

Today I challenge you to think on just one short verse from the longest chapter in the Bible. Take a few moments to memorize my paraphrase of Psalm 119:92. Then meditate on it throughout your day.

How could I ever forget to cling to Your Word?
For it has been my lifeline!

THURSDAY
FINISH WELL!
Reading of the Day: I Samuel 10:6-11; 13:11-14

"The Spirit of the Lord will come powerfully upon
you, and you will prophesy with them;
and you will be changed into a different person."
I Samuel 10:6 (words of Samuel to Saul)

God changed Saul's heart.
I Samuel 10:9

Saul started out so well. He was wise and innocent—perhaps timid and a bit cowardly—but powerful and prophetic when filled with God's Spirit. God changed his heart and gave him a wonderful start as king. Saul truly was changed into another man. Sadly, though, he then changed into yet another man who balked against the Lord.

My e-mentor, Win, set an example for me in her daily prayer: 1) that her faith would never fail and 2) that God would continue to use her all the days of her life.

Let's not just start well… let's finish well!

FRIDAY
WHAT'S WRONG WITH IT?
Reading of the Day: I Samuel 14:7, 36-37, 40

What's wrong with doing what seems right?

It does not pay to be impatient with God. Look at the example of Saul. When Samuel did not show up within the expected time frame, he acted foolishly and proceeded to offer a sacrifice on his own instead of waiting for Samuel. The cost of his impatience? His kingship and the future of his descendants!

As Saul stumbles down the steep slope of disobedience and foolishness, we see a phrase repeated again and again in I Samuel 14. "Do what seems good to you." We can sure get into heaps of trouble if we simply do what seems good to us!

I challenge you today to take time to ask God what

seems good to HIM, even if it seems obvious to you what might be the good thing.

You never know what the cost of your foolishness might be.

SATURDAY
DOWN THE SLIPPERY SLOPE
Reading of the Day: I Samuel 15:19-29

As I was writing this entry, I was about to have a difficult conversation with someone. I wanted to control my emotions to lovingly say just what I needed to say, carefully choosing the right time, words, and way to communicate the truth in love.

As I read I Samuel 15 that day, Saul's example was a challenge to me to obey fully by speaking the truth in love as the Scriptures tell us.

Saul crashed at the bottom of the hill after descending the slippery slope of disobedience. Like a child, he defended himself, blamed others, made excuses, and then finally begged for mercy. You can almost hear the child in him, pulling on Samuel's robe and wailing,

"I have sinned, but *please!*
Honor me now before the elders!"
I Samuel 15:30

Avoid the slippery slope. Choose the godly course of action today.

SUNDAY
DEFINITION OF OBEDIENCE
Reading of the Day: I Samuel 15:30-35

Today we reach the conclusion of the effective phase of Saul's reign. Sadly, he continued on and on in a relentless cycle of failure and disobedience. When Saul begged Samuel to change his mind, Samuel replied,

> "The Glory of Israel does not lie or
> change His mind."
> I Samuel 15:29

At the conclusion of the chapter, we read these sad words:

> "Samuel did not see Saul again until the day of his
> death; for Samuel grieved over Saul.
> And the Lord regretted that He had made Saul
> king over Israel."

When our kids were little, we taught them that obedience means

> to do *what* you are told, *when* you are told,
> and with a *good attitude*.

We would do well to heed that same advice!

MONDAY
A DIFFERENT "IF IT SEEMS GOOD TO YOU..."
Reading of the Day: I Chronicles 13:1-4

Remember the phrase that is repeated many times in I Samuel 13 and 14?

"Do what seems good to you."

In contrast to King Saul, David was a man after God's own heart. In 1 Chronicles 13:2, you can find a similar phrase spoken by King David to all the assembly of Israel, "If it seems good to you..."

But this time there is an important modifier.

*"If it seems good to you **and if it is from the Lord our God**, let us..."*

Factor God highly into the equation of your life's direction today!

TUESDAY
GOD USES SMALL STONES
Reading of the Day: Look up the context of the two verses quoted below

"I have sinned. I violated the Lord's command and your instructions.

I was afraid of the men and so I gave in to them."
(Saul's words in I Samuel 15:24)

"The Lord who rescued me from the paw of the
lion and the paw of the bear
will rescue me from the hand of this Philistine."
(David's words in I Samuel 17:37)

David's bravery makes an outstanding contrast to Saul's cowardice. But it wasn't David's bravery that killed Goliath. It was his great trust in a trustworthy God. My brother Vito often writes to me to say that God can use one small stone to kill a giant.

"Then he…picked up five smooth stones."
1 Samuel 17:40

Prayer for today:

*Lord, I pray that you make me a person
of brave faith like young David.
Just like you used that small, smooth stone in his
sling, use me today!*

WEDNESDAY
CONTINUE IN WORSHIP
Reading of the Day: Psalm 100

Woody and I once attended a Free Church of Scotland while we were in London. There were several things about the service that impacted us, but what struck us most was the first phrase uttered by the pastor, "Let us continue in worship."

What a great thought! We don't go to a church service to begin to worship; we go to *continue* in worship.

I trust you began your day by worshiping God. As you continue in worship today, think on these words from Brother Lawrence,

> *As I go about the rest of my day, may I continue in*
> *familiar conversation with You,*
> *imploring Your grace, offering You all my actions.*

THURSDAY
ALTERNATIVE ENERGY
Reading of the Day: Philippians 2:12-18

> "Be energetic in your life of salvation,
> reverent and sensitive before God.
> That energy is God's energy,
> an energy deep within you,
> God himself willing and working at what
> will give him the most pleasure."
> Philippians 2:13 The Message

What a most excellent thought for today! This passage challenges you to be energetic in your life of salvation. That energy comes from deep within you, welling up from a divine source. It gives us the will and the way to do what brings Him the most pleasure.

Make this your prayer today:

May I be reverent and sensitive before You today, God.
Help me tap into that energy source
You provide deep within.
Give me a passion for being and doing
what brings You pleasure!
That's what I want my life to be all about.

FRIDAY
APPLY GOD'S WORD TO PRAYER
Reading of the Day: Isaiah 40:28-31
(Try to read it from at least two versions)

One day in Costa Rica, I was taking my morning Celestial Prayer Walk. That day I prayed fervently from Isaiah 40, sensing a special need for His strength. As I walked and prayed, I ran across the campus gardener, Tulio, who was facing many trials at that time. So, I paused to pray aloud with him from today's passage, which I had written on a card to carry with me.

"You, my Lord, are the everlasting God, the
Creator of the ends of the earth.
You will not grow tired or weary, and Your understanding no one can fathom.

You give strength to the weary and
increase the power of the weak.
Even youths grow tired and weary,
and young men stumble and fall;
but when I hope in You, O, Lord,
my strength will be renewed.
I will soar on wings like eagles;
I will run and not grow weary,
I will walk and not faint." *(Su's paraphrase)*

I challenge you to pray Isaiah 40:28-31 for yourself
now, and be open to praying it over someone else
during the course of your day.

SATURDAY
T.H.I.N.K.
Reading of the Day: James 3:1-6

"No one can tame the tongue." So writes James.
And, sadly, each of us has proven that true time
and again. So, for the next several days I want to
challenge you to T.H.I.N.K. before you speak.

True. Helpful. Inspiring. Necessary. Kind.
T.H.I.N.K.

Learn to run your conversation through the
T.H.I.N.K. filter, and you will begin to please God
more consistently as you honor Him with your
tongue.

Make Colossians 4:6 into a personalized prayer today:

May my speech always be with grace,
seasoned, as it were, with salt...

SUNDAY
T.H.I.N.K.
"T" IS FOR TRUTH
Reading of the Day: Psalm 34:11-14

"Keep your tongue from evil and your lips
from speaking lies."
Psalm 34:13

In court, one is called on to swear "to tell the truth,
the whole truth and nothing but the truth." That's not
always as simple as it sounds. The movie, *The Whole
Truth,* points out that revealing a portion of the truth
can paint a very different picture than telling the whole
truth. (I'm not recommending the movie, by the way!)

God is a God of truth. In Proverbs 6:16-17, a lying
tongue is listed along with hands that shed innocent blood. God takes the truth seriously. Make it
your goal today to align your speech with the truth.

Remember today **"T is for TRUTH."** And make
this your prayer:

Lord, help me feel the same way about truth as You do!

MONDAY
T.H.I.N.K.
"H" IS FOR HELPFUL
Reading of the Day: Proverbs 16:20-24

"Pleasant words are a honeycomb."
Proverbs 16:24a

"The lips of the righteous nourish many."
Proverbs 10:21

If my words are going to be helpful, they must feed the hearers, develop their character, and nudge them in the right direction in the challenging journey of life.

Make this prayer your own today:

Father, help my words to be like honey today. I want to instruct and encourage others, helping them to live a life that is pleasing to You. Help me to say only what is helpful. Help me listen to Your Holy Spirit so that I might choose words that nourish others.

TUESDAY
T.H.I.N.K.
"I" IS FOR INSPIRING
Reading of the Day: Proverbs 15:26-33

"Encourage one another and build each other up."
I Thessalonians 5:11 New Living Translation

Mark Twain once said, "I can live for two months on a good compliment." As Christians, we should be experts at seeing the spark of God's creation in each person. Our words should encourage and inspire others around us. Proverbs exhorts us that our good word will make a heart glad. How can you make a heart glad today? We are all in the building business… the "building each other up" business!

Here's a suggested prayer for today as you THINK about your words being INSPIRING:

> *Help me today, Lord, to see the opportunities*
> *You graciously give me*
> *to build others up with my words.*
> *When people don't treat me right,*
> *help me see the grain of good,*
> *and cheer them on with an encouraging word.*

WEDNESDAY
T.H.I.N.K
"N" IS FOR NECESSARY
Reading of the Day: Ephesians 5:1-4

"If you don't have anything nice to say,
don't say anything at all."
"Instead remind each other of
God's goodness and be thankful."
Ephesians 5:4 The Living Bible

God has created us to be creative. Strive to make your conversations creative, fun, interesting, and intentional. Instead of falling into patterns of criticism and sarcasm, try to draw people into conversations that build relationships and that will matter for now and eternity.

Lord, help me to have spontaneous, yet purposeful,
conversations with people today.
Help me convey Your goodness and faithfulness to
others in the conversations
I am privileged to enjoy today.

THURSDAY
T.H.I.N.K.
"K" IS FOR KINDNESS
Reading of the Day: Proverbs 15:1-4

"A gentle answer turns away wrath, but a harsh
word stirs up anger."
Proverbs 15:1

My harsh words are often effective.

Effective, that is, in prompting self-defeat, distancing people from me, and distancing myself and others from my Lord. The times I manage to respond with a *gentle* answer, I am at peace with God and myself, and others see in me something different ... *Someone* different! It's rarely my intention to speak harshly, but sometimes my words can feel like sand-paper to the hearer.

Throw away the sandpaper today, and make this your prayer:

Convict me, Lord, of harsh words.
Give me a spirit of gentleness and humility.
Allow me to THINK before speaking, and utter only
words of kindness.

FRIDAY
NO MORE BONDAGE FOR ME!
Reading of the Day: Acts 15:6-11

"It is for freedom that Christ has set us free.
Stand firm, then, and
do not let yourselves be burdened again
by a yoke of slavery."
Galatians 5:1

The first step on the way to victory is
to recognize the enemy.
—Corrie Ten Boom

One of the things I most admire about the writings and life story of Corrie Ten Boom is that she could have held on to bitterness for the life stolen from her by Hitler and the Nazis. Yet, she recognized that there is a captivity worse than a concentration camp.

God does not address non-issues, so He wouldn't have warned us not to return to bondage if it weren't a possibility. These days we rarely hear teaching about bondage and slavery, except in terms of world-wide human trafficking and slavery. Who is your true enemy? What is holding you in captivity?

Even as a Christian, you might have a harness of slavery on you—fear, bitterness, pride, impure thoughts, or materialism. There are countless forms of bondage. Pray that God would reveal to you any stronghold holding you hostage. Christ has set you free to live a free life!

Lord, help me recognize the true enemies
in my life today that
Keep me from the abundant life You offer.

SATURDAY
A LESSON FROM THE LIFE OF DAVID
Reading of the Day: I Samuel 30:1-6

Just before King Saul was killed, and while David and his band of mighty men were living in Ziklag, the Amalekites raided their town and took all their goods along with their wives and children. When David and his men returned home from serving in Achish's army and found their families gone and the town up in smoke, David's men were embittered against him and spoke of stoning him. Understandably, David was "greatly distressed."

"But David found strength in the Lord his God."
I Samuel 30:6

Unlike Saul, who was allowed by God to perish "because he did not inquire of the Lord," David inquired of the Lord. (I Chronicles 10:14, I Samuel 30:7-8)

If you are facing distress, look to David's example today. Inquire of Him and…

Strengthen yourself in the Lord.

SUNDAY
WHEN THERE'S NO ONE
TO TURN TO
Reading of the Day: John 15:9-17

Imagine being continually and cruelly rejected by your own people. Your efforts to love them are met by indifference and even intense hatred. Ponder awakening each morning to the reality that there is a plot to kill you. One of your closest associates will betray you and hand you over to be killed. Your most vocal supporter will deny even knowing you, and all your other friends will desert you. Your own brothers will misunderstand and mock you. You have no friend to turn to.

Jesus faced all this with peace and joy. He longs to give you the same.

> **"Peace** I leave with you; my **peace** I give you.
> I do not give to you as the world gives.
> Do not let your hearts be troubled
> and do not be afraid."
> John 14:27

> "I have told you this so that my **joy** may be in you
> and that your **joy** may be complete."
> John 15:11

MONDAY
MORE THAN YOU CAN MUSTER
Reading of the Day: Mark 9:16-24

> "You are my witnesses," declares the LORD, "and
> my servant whom I have chosen,
> so that you may know and believe me and
> understand that I am he."
> Isaiah 43:10

This verse says we will not only *know* God, but will also *believe* Him! Trusting an invisible God does not come naturally, and God knows that well! Jesus said to Thomas, "The people who have faith in me without seeing me are the ones who are really blessed." John 20:29

Trust grows only by stepping out in faith and intentionally *choosing* to trust. It doesn't grow because of a gradually increasing warm, fuzzy feeling. Sometimes taking a step of trust requires more than we can muster. But Jesus' example of compassion for the boy and his father in Mark 9 shows clearly that God is anxious to help us overcome our unbelief.

TUESDAY
NO WORRIES!
Reading of the Day: Luke 10:38-42

"As Jesus and his disciples were on their way,
he came to a village where a woman named
Martha opened her home to him."
Luke 10:38

Note that it was *Martha*, not *Mary*, who invited Jesus into their home. Jesus loved to frequent the home of Mary, Martha and Lazarus because he loved them, and they were gracious hosts. When Jesus rebuked Martha, it was out of care and concern for her frenzied state.

"Martha, Martha," the Lord answered, "you are
worried and upset about many things,
but only one thing is needed." (v. 41)

Both Mary and Martha were lovers of God and were loved by Jesus. As Charles Spurgeon put it, "They were both women of a choice spirit… Martha was a most estimable and earnest woman, a true believer, and an ardent follower of Jesus whose joy it was to entertain Jesus at the house of which she was the mistress." Martha's intent was to honor Christ, and He did not disapprove of her service, only of her worries and fretting.

He accepts us as His children and loves us so much that He would never sentence us to serve Him with an anxious and distracted mind.

WEDNESDAY
WHAT DOES IT MEAN TO WAIT?
Reading of the Day: Romans 8:18-25

"[Martha] had a sister called Mary,
who sat at the Lord's feet listening to what he said."
Luke 10:39

There is an interesting parallel between the Luke passage about Mary and Martha and the portion you read today from Romans 8. Both talk about waiting. "To wait" seems so dull, boring, and unbearable – anything but dynamic! Romans 8 paints a colorful idea of what it means to wait. Look back at today's passage, and note the verbs and adjectives that add life to the concept of waiting.

When Jesus was a guest of Martha and Mary, He

commended Mary, not because she was idle, but because she was waiting, listening to Him, still, willing to do whatever He desired. Waiting doesn't mean dull inactivity. It means a life of obedient faith which results in a life of eternal significance.

"Mary has chosen what is better,
and it will not be taken away from her."
Luke 10:42

THURSDAY
HEAVENLY MAGIC MARKER
Reading of the Day: Malachi 3:16-18

"Then those who feared the LORD talked with
each other, and the LORD listened and heard.
A scroll of remembrance was written in his presence
concerning those who feared the LORD and
honored his name."
Malachi 3:16

What an amazing scene! Just imagine talking with others who share your fear of the Lord, while God Himself listens carefully. Because you and your friends fear and honor Him, the Heavenly Scribe carefully notes everything you have to say.

Our words can actually merit being recorded on heavenly scrolls if we fear Him and honor His name! And just think of the wonder of verse 17: that God might be thinking of *you*, saying, "_____ is mine and is part of my treasured possession!"

May your life merit the use of a heavenly magic marker today!

FRIDAY
COLD AND SLOTHFUL
Reading of the Day: Proverbs 19:15-21

"Laziness brings on deep sleep,
and the shiftless go hungry."
Proverbs 19:15

I was struck a couple of years back by à Kempis' thoughts, expressing that we do not allow truth to pierce our hearts because we still love the pleasures of the senses.

*So fixed are our spirits in slothfulness
and cold indifference
that we seldom overcome so much as one evil habit.*
—Thomas à Kempis

*A sluggish, dawdling, and dilatory man
may have spasms of activity,
but he never acts continuously and consecutively
with energetic quickness.*
—George Stillman Hillard

I don't know about you, but I don't want to be identified as sluggish, dawldling, dilatory, cold *or* slothful!

SATURDAY
TRUE HOPE
Reading of the Day: Romans 5:3-5

I am pleased to include the following entry from my daughter, Krista Ophus. Krista is a school teacher in Chicago and she and her family are planting a church in their neighborhood of South Lawndale in Chicago. Here are Krista's words:

Have you ever had a day when you thought nothing more could go wrong? One day, within 24 hours, my son broke his leg, all the pipes burst in our house, and our car broke down. From the first spill of coffee in the morning, you sometimes know it's going to be one of those days! Maybe it's not just a day, but a year full of tragedies, struggles, and not seeing any step forward.

I've worked in situations where I felt I've done everything in my human power, crying out to God and not seeing any response… at least not the response I wanted. As I strive to follow Christ in situations beyond my control, that suffering produces perseverance. Sticking with my Savior, even through the tears and struggles, produces character.

That character produces hope, and not the kind that says, "I hope that job situation changes," or, "I hope you feel better"... but a real hope that does not fail. I will not be put to shame because I have hope in my Savior, hope in His words that are true. I know the ending - where He will take all wrongs and make them right.

If you find yourself in "one of those days," hang on to hope! Rest on the fact that God's eternal plan is always going right.

There is hope! True hope!

SUNDAY
FIRST DAILY TREASURE
Reading of the Day: Psalm 84:1-7

Let's focus for the next few days on benefits we enjoy when we walk daily with God. The first benefit is:

THE DAILY TREASURE OF HIS STRENGTH

I don't know about you, but I am weak! I need a supernatural resource of strength each new day. In the midst of the distress of the nation of Israel, Isaiah cried out to God on behalf of his people,

"Be our strength every morning."
Isaiah 33:2

Abide in Him, and find your strength in Him today. Then you will benefit from this promise,

"Blessed are those whose strength is in you, who
have set their hearts on pilgrimage...
They go from strength to strength."
Psalm 84:5,7

MONDAY
THE DAILY TREASURE OF HIS PRESENCE
Reading of the Day: Hebrews 13:5-8

"God is there, ready to help;
I'm fearless no matter what.
Who or what can get to me?"
Hebrews 13:5b The Message

Once I was traveling alone to the US during my "Balrog years" (the term we use to describe the trials of 2010-2014). I was crying out to God for help as I boarded the full flight. I decided if I was serious about seeking Him with my whole heart, that I would dedicate the flight time to prayer and God's Word. Amazingly, at my side I had one of the only empty seats. Not long after takeoff, I sensed God's voice saying to me, "See that empty seat? I'm sitting in it right next to you." The treasure of His presence warmed my heart and infused peace in my soul.

Upon arrival at my destination, my brother Vito texted me, saying, "I have been praying that you would know that God is sitting right next to you on that plane."

That can't be a coincidence!

> Watch for the "empty seats"
> beside you throughout your day.
> Write a Post-it-Note to remind you,
> "I'm right here beside you."

TUESDAY
THE DAILY TREASURE OF HIS PRESENCE – PART 2
Reading of the Day: John 14:15-21

When we begin our walk with God, we step out in faith like a leap in the dark. We cannot see where this path will lead us or the face of the One leading us. It can seem almost like a struggle between human reason and craziness. But that's where complete trust comes into the picture.

When Jesus was on earth, he assured his disciples time and again that they would not be alone.

"I will talk to the Father, and he'll provide you another Friend so that you will always have someone with you. This Friend is the Spirit of Truth.

The godless world can't take him in because it
doesn't have eyes to see him,
doesn't know what to look for.
But you know him already because he has been
staying with you,
and will even be *in* you!"
John 14:15-17 The Message

His presence accompanies us, comforts us, encourages us, feeds us, and gives us the strength and
help to continue our walk of faith.

WEDNESDAY
THE GIFT OF GENTLE LISTENING
Reading of the Day: I Samuel 20:1-9

Though Jonathan had no inkling of his father Saul's
fierce jealousy and desire to kill his dear friend
David, he *did* listen to his friend, willing to put his
life on the line for David.

How can we show grace to one another as friends?
Anne Lamott puts it well when she writes,

"We communicate grace to one another by holding space for people when they are hurt or terrified,
instead of trying to fix them, or manage their emotions for them. We offer ourselves as silent companionship, or gentle listening when someone feels
very alone."

"Always be prepared to give an answer
to everyone who asks you
to give the reason for the hope that you have.
But do this with gentleness and respect."
I Peter 3:15-16

Give someone the gift of "holding space," offering silent companionship and gentle listening.

THURSDAY
THE JOY OF THE LORD IS YOUR STRENGTH!
Reading of the Day: Nehemiah 8:1-12

If I could go back in time, I'd love to experience the Great Revival under the prophet Ezra described in Nehemiah 8. God's Word was so alive and fresh. The people gathered "as one man" (v. 1) before the newly erected gates of Jerusalem. As Ezra opened God's book, the people all stood. They lifted their hands, crying, "Amen! Amen!" as "Ezra blessed the Lord and great God." (v. 6) Then they all bowed low, faces to the ground, and worshiped God. The scriptures were read, translated, and explained clearly. The people wept as their hearts were touched. (v. 9)

It was in this context that Nehemiah declared,

"Do not be grieved, for the joy of the Lord is your strength!"

Lord, revive us today with a fresh touch of Your Word!

FRIDAY
COVENANT PRAYER
Reading of the Day: John 17:6-19

The following is a prayer adapted by John Wesley for use in what were called "covenant services." The first recorded covenant service was held in France in 1755 with 1,800 people present. There John Wesley presented this prayer as a renewal of commitment to God.

Seriously consider personalizing the modernized version of the prayer quoted below.

> *I am no longer my own, but Yours.*
> *Put me to what You will, rank me with whom You will;*
> *Put me to doing, put me to suffering;*
> *Let me be employed for You or laid aside for You,*
> *Exalted for You or laid low for You;*
> *Let me be full, let me be empty;*
> *Let me have all things, let me have nothing;*
> *I freely and heartily yield all things to Your pleasure and disposal.*

> "You are not your own; you
> were bought at a price.
> Therefore honor God with your body."
> I Corinthians 6:19-20

SATURDAY
SORTING OUT THE ESSENTIAL
Reading of the Day: Romans 6:1-9

Death is rather a taboo subject in the USA. But it's a subject you can't get around in the Bible! Take these excerpts from Romans 6 as a prime example:

"Now if we **died** with Christ, we believe that we will also live with him.
For we know that since Christ was raised from the **dead**, he cannot **die** again;
death no longer has mastery over him.
The **death** he **died**, he **died** to sin once for all; but the life he lives, he lives to God."

That chapter refers to death twenty times, concluding that "the wages of sin is **death**, but the gift of God is eternal life in Christ Jesus our Lord."

Evidence of death is all around us, try hard as we may to ignore it. I don't want to be morbid, but I ask you to think today on the emphasis in Romans 6, keeping in mind this quote from Gary Thomas:

Death acts like a filter, helping us hold on to the essential and let go of the trivial.

Live your life today letting go of the trivial, so you have your hands free to hold onto the essential.

SUNDAY
ALIGN YOUR PRIORITIES
Reading of the Day: Romans 6:10-18

"In the same way, count yourselves dead to sin but
alive to God in Christ Jesus."
Romans 6:11

Humor me one more day as I conclude thoughts
about why the subject of death is important to address. As Gary Thomas' quote from yesterday implied, considering the eventuality of death reminds
us of the things that are important in life.

*When we schedule our priorities and follow our
passions without regarding eternity,
we are essentially looking into the wrong
end of a telescope.
Instead of seeing things more clearly, our vision
becomes tunneled and distorted.*
—Gary Thomas

*Help me, Lord, today to see my life
from an eternal perspective.
Align my priorities with the things that
are most important in life!*

MONDAY
THE STRENGTH OF MY HEART
Reading of the Day: Psalm 73:21-16

As I write this entry, I've been going through a year-and-a-half-long health crisis which has deeply impacted our lives. Surprisingly, I don't often ask myself the question, "Why?" The question I ask more often is, "What am I learning from this?"

If I were asked to distill my thoughts on what I've learned so far in this trial, it would be the simple truth that life boils down to trust or despair. I choose to trust. God is worthy of my trust. Simply choosing to trust each moment, when I cannot understand, somehow gives glory to God. That's what my life is about… not me; not things making sense; but giving glory to God.

Make these verses into the cry of your heart today, just as I have made them my own:

> "Whom have I in heaven but you?
> And earth has nothing I desire besides you.
> My flesh and my heart may fail,
> But God is the strength of my heart
> And my portion forever."
> Psalm 73:25-26

TUESDAY
DELIBERATE PURSUIT
Reading of the Day: Hebrews 12:1-6

"Therefore, since we are surrounded by such a
great cloud of witnesses,
let us throw off everything that hinders
and the sin that so easily entangles,
and let us run with perseverance the
race marked out for us."
Hebrews 12:1

I've been impacted by the book *Crazy Love* by
Francis Chan. We will never really make it in our
daily struggle to be "devoted enough" to God.
Trying hard just doesn't cut it! Chan writes, "Slowly
I've learned to pray for God's help, and He has become my greatest love and desire." You don't grow
closer to God by simply living life; it requires delib-
erate pursuit and attentiveness.

There is so much more to life than what we see.
Live today as if it were the last day of your life, as
though people would remember today's words being your last.

Let the cloud of witnesses cheer you on!

WEDNESDAY
WHAT SHOULD I ASK FOR?
Reading of the Day: I Kings 3:5-10

I don't believe we need to get too worried about what we should pray for. After all, if you are talking to someone you know and trust, do you agonize over what you will talk about or ask him for?

That being said, it's still worth our while to look for what pleases God according to His Word. Solomon is one of the best examples.

"So give your servant a discerning heart to govern your people and to distinguish between right and wrong. For who is able to govern this great people of yours?"
I Kings 3:9

"The Lord was pleased that Solomon had asked for this." (v. 10)

What will you ask for today that will please God?

THURSDAY
CHOOSE TO FORGET
Reading of the Day: Philippians 3:12-14

"But one thing I do: Forgetting what is behind and straining toward what is ahead…"
Philippians 3:13

It often seems like our memories don't serve us well—they keep dredging up what we want to *forget* (like the Monkees' song that *constantly* pops into my mind and I wish I'd never heard!).

On the other hand, we struggle to recall what we desperately need to *remember* ("What was it I needed to do this morning?!?")

When forgetting seems impossible—we can *choose* moment by moment not to remember. Choose to forget what lies behind and to remember the goal of the prize for which God has called us heavenward.

Lord, help me to forget the things I should forget and to remember what I should remember.

FRIDAY
FALL AFRESH ON ME!
Reading of the Day: II Corinthians 3:12-18

"Now the Lord is the Spirit, and where the Spirit
of the Lord is, there is freedom.
And we, who with unveiled faces
all reflect the Lord's glory,
are being transformed into his likeness
with ever-increasing glory,
which comes from the Lord, who is the Spirit."
II Corinthians 3:17-18

Make this your prayer today:

Oh Father, You have placed your Spirit in me. Where your Spirit is there is freedom—freedom to look to You and to receive Your love and grace; freedom to submit to Your ongoing transformation. Help me to do just that. May I look and live more like Jesus with each passing year. May I give myself, and keep giving myself, to the things that are closest to Your heart. Spirit of the Living God, fall afresh on me!

SATURDAY
FOLLOWING DANIEL'S EXAMPLE
(See Instructions Below Before Reading!)
Reading of the Day: Daniel 9:4-19

As you read the passage for today, make the concepts into your own personal prayer, praying for yourself as well as your nation and society. I'll give a short example of my own prayer below, based on one of the most powerful examples of a man of prayer, Daniel.

What an awesome and great God You are! I rejoice in Your faithfulness because I know You will always keep Your loving promises. Humbly I come to You, well aware of my own sinfulness. When I see the news and the lives of those around me, I am so saddened by the sinfulness of this world. At the same time, though, I realize my own great sinfulness and know we are all one big, mixed-up world, and we're in such a mess because we've turned our backs on You! You are so righteous and just, and we are deserving of the disasters we face. But I also know that You are forgiving and merciful, so we can call on You, and You will listen and respond to our cries. I don't call out to You because I deserve help, but only because of Your mercy. Oh, Lord, listen! We need You! Forgive us, heal, and act!

SUNDAY
GUILTY AS CHARGED!
Reading of the Day: Daniel 6:1-12

Here are some words of Scripture describing the character of Daniel:

- He had an extraordinary spirit. (v. 3)

- He was faithful, without negligence or corruption. (v. 4)

- Even before he was in trouble, he continually knelt three times a day, praying and giving thanks to God. (v. 10)

- He constantly served God. (v. 16)

- While the king worried and cried out with a troubled voice, Daniel spoke with peace and calm. (v. 20, 21)

- He trusted in his God. (v. 23)

Daniel's enemies could find no fault in him except that he prayed faithfully to his God. Daniel pled, "Guilty as charged!"

May you and I be found guilty today of praying faithfully, just like Daniel!

MONDAY
ALL BACKBONE
Reading of the Day: Daniel 6:13-28

"At this, the administrators and the satraps
tried to find grounds for charges
against Daniel in his conduct of government
affairs, but they were unable to do so.
They could find no corruption in him,
because he was trustworthy and neither corrupt
nor negligent."
Daniel 6:4

I love a comment written in the margin of my Bible. It's a quote from Betty McGehee from the women's retreat at Sandy Creek Bible Camp in Washington on the Brazos, Texas, from May 10, 1990.

"The reason the lions didn't eat Daniel is that he was all backbone."

Lord, help me be all backbone today!

TUESDAY
GOD'S UNFAILING LOVE
Reading of the Day: Psalm 143:1-6

> "Let the morning bring me word of
> your unfailing love,
> For I have put my trust in you.
> Show me the way I should go,
> for to you I lift up my soul."
> Psalm 143:8

We'll take two days to meditate on the verse above. Write it on a card or Post-it-Note, so you can look at it often. Here are some questions to ask God which might help you get a jump start on meditating right now:

- What does it mean that your love is unfailing?

- Have I experienced that kind of love from You? In what ways have I...or haven't I?

- Do I *need* your unfailing love?

- Do I really believe that?

- Really?

- Do I live in a way that reflects Your unfailing love to the world around me?

WEDNESDAY
SHOW ME THE WAY
Reading of the Day: Psalm 143:7-12

"If you wake me each morning with the
sound of your loving voice,
I'll go to sleep each night trusting in you.
Point out the road I must travel;
I'm all ears, all eyes before you."
Psalm 143:8 The Message

Continue to review the verse I asked you to write
out yesterday. (If you didn't do it yesterday, there's
still time!) Ask yourself the following questions as
you meditate on Psalm 143:8.

- How am I doing with trusting?

- What elements of my life do I need to entrust to God? What have I held back from
  Him?

- How have I been trusting myself more
  than trusting God?

- What should trust look and feel like in my
  life?

- "Show me the way I should go." How does
  my independence or pride resist this?

- Do I want to know what way I should go?
  Am I willing to obey?

- Are there things God has revealed to me about the way I should go that I have not followed, instead choosing my own way?

THURSDAY
RIGHTEOUS SACRIFICE:
TAKE MY EYES
Reading of the Day: Psalm 51:14-19

"Then there will be righteous sacrifices…"
Psalm 51:19

Righteous sacrifices are legitimate and proper, sacrifices that are appropriate because they are offered in the right spirit and right relationship with God. Over the next few days, we'll give God, one by one, our "body parts." Today, start with your eyes, prayerfully giving to Him each element you can think of that has to do with your sight, including the following prayers.

LORD, TAKE MY EYES…

- May I place before Your eyes only what pleases You.

- May my eyes see people as You see them.

- May my eyes notice Your gifts of creation and cause me to praise You.

- May my eyes not lust after that which You do not intend for me…whatever that might be!

(Try to remember this key word throughout your day:
EYES!)

FRIDAY
TAKE MY EARS
Reading of the Day: Revelation 3:19-22

The Bible speaks a lot about hearing. The short "Reading of the Day" passage in Revelation 3 refers to hearing twice:

- If anyone hears my voice…

- He who has ears to hear, let him hear.

Hearing is a critical part of your spiritual walk and righteous sacrifice. Take a few minutes to pray through the following bullet points. Don't just read them! Pray them from your heart!

- May I hear Your voice.

- May I listen to teaching and worship that would build me up.

- May I hear the heart cries of people in need of Christ.

LORD, TAKE MY EARS!
(Try to remember this key word throughout your day:
EARS!)

SATURDAY
TAKE MY MOUTH
Reading of the Day: James 3:7-12

"Lord, open my lips and my mouth
will declare your praise."
Psalm 51:15

The Scripture clearly indicates the most difficult righteous sacrifice you can offer is your tongue. Take a moment to think and pray about how God might use your tongue today for His honor.

LORD, TAKE MY MOUTH.

- May I speak words of encouragement and blessing.

- Put a guard over my mouth, Lord, that I would not be:

  - Critical

  - Harsh

  - Boasting

  - Exaggerating

(Try to remember this key word throughout your day:
MOUTH!)

SUNDAY
TAKE MY VOICE
Reading of the Day: Psalm 96

"Sing God a brand-new song!
Earth and everyone in it, sing!
Sing to God—worship God! Sing God a brand-
new song! Earth and everyone in it, sing!
Sing to God—worship God! Bravo, God, Bravo!
Everyone join in the great shout: Encore!"
Excerpts from Psalm 96 The Message

LORD, TAKE MY VOICE.

May I sing Your praises and declare Your glories.

If you can, take a moment to sing this great, old hymn:

> *Take my **voice** and let me sing*
> *Always, only for my King*
> *Take my lips and let them be filled with messages*
> *for Thee.*

(Try to remember this key word throughout your day:
VOICE!)

MONDAY
TAKE MY HANDS
Reading of the Day: Matthew 5:17-30

Today's reading speaks about cutting off your hand. Let me promise you, I'm not asking you to cut off your hands for today's righteous sacrifice! But I do ask that you take a moment to think of how you might use your hands today for God's glory.

LORD, TAKE MY HANDS.

Make them useful in your service to:

- Create

- Work

- Clean

- Type

- Embrace

- Reach out to people

May they be lifted in praise to You!

(Try to remember this key word throughout your day:
HANDS!)

TUESDAY
TAKE MY FEET
Reading of the Day: Isaiah 52:7-12

The more ready we are to move with the gospel,
the more life and power and joy and security we will
know in the gospel.
—John Piper

Once Woody and I played a version of the old show, "The Newlywed's Game," where I had to identify my husband's bare feet peeking from under a sheet along with the feet of many other men in our church. It was a very simple task for me to recognize Woody's size 13 foot with a thick, discolored nail on his big toe.

Not many of us boast of our lovely feet, but today I'm calling on you to have beautiful feet! Feet represent a readiness to move from one place to another. Ephesians 6:15 says our shoes are specially fitted with the readiness that comes from the gospel of peace.

Where do you expect your feet to take you today? Entrust those activities to God right now, before you even do them. And think *prayerfully* of a way you can honor Him with this sacrifice today.

LORD, TAKE MY FEET.

Strengthen them to:

- Run from evil and run toward something constructive and good

- Be ready with the message of the gospel as the opportunity arises

- Run errands for others

- Be still and REST a moment as well, for Your glory!

(Try to remember this key word throughout your day:
FEET!)

WEDNESDAY
IT'S THE HEART THAT COUNTS!
Reading of the Day: II Chronicles 6:1-11

I think it is possible for God to deny your heart-felt prayer request, but at that same time take delight in your plea.

When Solomon gave his dedication speech for the Temple, he said,

"My father David had it in his heart to build a
temple for the Name of the LORD,
the God of Israel. But the LORD
said to my father David,

'Because it was in your heart to
build a temple for my Name,
you did well to have this in your heart.
Nevertheless, you are not the one to build the
temple...'"
II Chronicles 6:7-8

I don't know about you, but I would like to learn to
pray for what pleases God—if not the request itself,
at least my heart attitude behind the request. Make
it your prayer right now that the essence of your
prayers and petitions before Him would bring Him
satisfaction and joy.

THURSDAY
HE KNOWS YOUR HEART
Reading of the Day: II Chronicles 6:26-31

As Solomon continued his humble plea before God
and His people at the dedication of the Temple, he
prayed,

"When a prayer or plea is made by
any of your people Israel—
each one aware of his afflictions and pains, and
spreading out his hands toward this temple- then
hear from heaven, your dwelling place.
Forgive, and deal with each man
according to all he does,

since you know his heart
(for you alone know the hearts of men)."
II Chronicles 6:29-30

How awesome that God longs to have us share our own personal afflictions and pains! Not only that, but God will deal with each of us in a very personal way, because He knows the hearts of men. Take a moment to spread out your hands to God, sharing today's concerns with Him and thanking Him that He knows your heart.

FRIDAY
RELENTLESS WAVES
Reading of the Day: Isaiah 40:11-18

"When you pass through the waters,
I will be with you;
And when you pass through the rivers,
they will not sweep over you."
Isaiah 43:2

During our second year living in Costa Rica, I almost drowned at Cahuita Beach. As I struggled to get to shore, I lost consciousness at least twice. Woody swam out to try to save me, but before long he felt sure we would both drown. If it weren't for God's intervention and Woody's strength, focus, and words of encouragement, I never would have survived. When I finally was able to stand near the shore, I passed out yet again in the water, face down. You cannot get much closer to death!

One recurrent thought I had during that harrowing experience was that the waves just never let up.

"Was it not you who dried up the waters
of the great deep,
who made a road in the depths of the sea so that
the redeemed might cross over?"
Isaiah 51:10

Do you ever feel like you are facing relentless, pounding waves as you are drowning in the sea? Call out to the One who measures the seas in the palm of His hand and can create a dry road for you in the waters of the great deep.

SATURDAY
NOT A LOSER
Reading of the Day: II Corinthians 7:2-7

If Paul could have great confidence in a bunch of losers like the Corinthians (forgive my harsh words about them), there is a lot of hope for you, for me, and for "black holes" – people who suck up time and energy but never yield results. Listen to some of these amazing phrases from

II Corinthians 7:

- Great is my confidence in you; great is my boasting on your behalf.

- [Titus] reported to us your longing, your mourning, your zeal for me.

- And besides our comfort, we rejoiced even much more for the joy of Titus, because his spirit has been refreshed by you all.

- I am glad I can have complete confidence in you.

Remember today that you are not a loser and neither are others around you. Be like Paul. Look for the grain of good in yourself and others.

SUNDAY
HELP ME!!
Reading of the Day: I Peter 5:6-11

Sometimes all I can do in my distress is call out, "Help me! Help me! Help me!" It may not sound very spiritual, but it's a call in the right direction. David called out to God morning, noon, and night.

"My thoughts trouble me and I am distraught.
My heart is in anguish within me.
Fear and trembling have beset me.
But I call to God, and the Lord saves me.

Evening, morning, and noon I cry out in distress
And He hears my voice.
Cast your cares on the Lord and He will sustain you;
He will never let the righteous fall.
But, as for me, I trust in You."
Psalm 55

In this psalm, David confessed he was beset with anguish, fear, trembling and distress. Those emotions were his call to cast his cares on the One who could sustain him and to confess his trust in the Lord, even as he muddled through his tangled emotions.

Don't be afraid to cast all your anxiety on Him, because He cares about you!

MONDAY
WHAT COMES NATURALLY
Reading of the Day: Matthew 14:13-21

"When Jesus landed and saw a large crowd,
he had compassion on them and healed their sick."
Matthew 14:14

Jesus reacted with what came most natural to Him: compassion and healing mercy. However, it's possible sometimes He exercises great restraint to work in another way. A plan of profound importance sometimes exists that overrides the miracle we desperately desire. It is comforting to know instantaneous healing and resurrection power come more naturally to Jesus than waiting and working through long, but necessary processes.

God is sovereign, and God is sweet. Trust Him—whether He works the miraculous or overrides the result you desire.

TUESDAY
GOT SUFFERING?
Reading of the Day: John 15:18-25

We may seek God, or we may seek ease,
but we cannot seek both.
The road we travel is anything but easy.
It is true that God loves us and has a wonderful plan
for our lives,
but it is equally true that the plan is often fraught
with tension and uncertainty,
and with emotional, spiritual, and physical pain.
—Gary Thomas

There is a church in San Jose, Costa Rica, that sports a sign saying:

End Your Suffering Here!

I don't suppose they would attract nearly as many people if the sign said:

Want suffering? Join us!

These thoughts at first might not seem very encouraging. But if you are facing tension, uncertainty, and pain, know that you may just be in the center of His will for you today!

"If they persecuted me, they will persecute you also."
John 15:20

WEDNESDAY
TINY PUSHES AND MIGHTY SHOVES
Reading of the Day: II John 3-6

I long to accomplish a great and noble task,
but it is my chief duty to accomplish humble tasks as
though they were great and noble.
The world is moved not only by the mighty
shoves of the heroes,
but also by the aggregate of the tiny pushes of each
honest worker.
—Helen Keller

How many of us long to hear the words from the Lord, "Well done, good and faithful servant"? We might think of these words as applying to the "big names in Christianity," godly leaders in the church, or even missionaries. In contrast, I think that there will be far more everyday people —people who love God, pay attention to the little things, and are obedient—who will hear these precious words from the Lord, "Well done!"

"And this is love: that we walk in obedience
to his commands.
As you have heard from the beginning,
his command is that you walk in love."
II John 6

THURSDAY
LEARN FROM OTHERS
Reading of the Day: II Timothy 3:10-17

"You, however, know all about my teaching, my
way of life, my purpose, faith,
patience, love, endurance, persecutions, sufferings...
But as for you, continue in what you have learned
and have become convinced of."
II Timothy 3:10-11

Before the five missionaries in Operation Auca
in Ecuador went unknowingly to their deaths in
1956, they sang:

We rest on Thee, our Shield and Defender!
We go not forth alone against the foe;
Strong in Thy strength, safe in Thy keeping tender,
We rest on Thee, and in Thy Name we go.

These men and their families inspired many to go
out to share the gospel around the world. They
were courageous, spiritual, adventurous, and acted
out of concern for the Waorani people, willing to

give their lives to share God's good news with them.

Learn from others' teaching and example. And live in such a way that others learn from your own teaching and example.

FRIDAY
MILLION MAN MARCH
Reading of the Day: II Chronicles 14:9-15

There was a "Million Man March" long before Louis Farrakhan! Back in King Asa's time, there was a vast army of men who came out to meet him from the land of Ethiopia. Maybe there weren't a million Cushites, but from the Israelites' perspective, there might as well have been.

II Chronicles 14 records Asa's moving prayer as he faced this incredibly large and powerful army:

"Then Asa called to the LORD his God and said, 'LORD, there is no one like you to help the powerless against the mighty.
Help us, O LORD our God, for we rely on you, and in your name we have come against this vast army.
O LORD, you are our God; do not let man prevail against you.'"
II Chronicles 14:11

The Lord routed the Ethiopians before Asa. No army is too powerful, even against those of us who are "powerless," for the Lord our God is worthy of our trust!

SATURDAY
STRENGTH FROM THE RIGHT SOURCE
Reading of the Day: II Chronicles 16:2-13

> "For the eyes of the LORD range
> throughout the earth
> to strengthen those whose hearts are
> fully committed to him."
> II Chronicles 16:9

King Asa was given clear instructions from the Lord. "And if you seek Him, He will let you find Him: but if you forsake Him, He will forsake you." (II Chronicles 15:2) The king and the people of Israel began well. They sought Him, and He let them find Him, and He took care of them.

When in a pinch, however, it seemed so much more practical to seek a strong army as an ally rather than the Lord. Asa chose Syria as an ally, forgetting the Lord promised to strengthen those whose hearts were fully committed to Him.

Seek strength from the right source!
He's watching out for you!

SUNDAY
TAKE PRIDE!
Reading of the Day: II Chronicles 17:1-10

"(Jehoshaphat) sought the God of his father and
followed his commands
rather than the practices of Israel."
II Chronicles 17:4

Two things are worth noting about this king:

1. He sent out officials throughout his kingdom to
    teach the people of Israel. (It's almost like he was
    obeying the Great Commission before it even
    existed!)

2. *He took great pride in the ways of the Lord.*
    (Those who are proud are reproved by God,
    but *this* kind of pride is one to aspire to.)

How can you take pride in the ways
of the Lord today?

MONDAY
WORD OF ENCOURAGEMENT?
Reading of the Day: I Peter 4:12-19

God's Word, the examples of Bible characters, and
the words and example of Christ show us that life
is full of difficulties. If our faith depended on life

turning out just as we'd dreamed, we would have good reason to be very disillusioned. But God "promises" us trials in life. Among many such promises is this "word of encouragement":

"And you have forgotten that *word of encouragement* that addresses you as sons:
'My son, do not make light of the Lord's discipline, and do not lose heart when he rebukes you.'"
Hebrews 12:5-6

If life isn't fair, if things don't turn out today like you'd wish, thank God that His promises and your hope are built on an unchanging, faithful God.

My hope is built on nothing less than
Jesus' blood and righteousness.

TUESDAY
THE BEST IS YET TO COME
Reading of the Day: I Peter 1:3-9

Our friends Suzie and Juan wear wedding bands inscribed with, "The best is yet to come." If they exchanged rings simply thinking that marital bliss was going to be a constant "up curve" on the graph of life, at some point they would experience disappointment. However, having been part of their wedding ceremony, I know their eyes are ultimately focused on eternity. With that perspective, it's reassuring to know that the best *is* yet to come!

"Because Jesus was raised from the dead,
we've been given a brand-new life and
have everything to live for,
including a future in heaven—and
the future starts now!
God is keeping careful watch over us and the future.
The Day is coming when you'll have it all—life
healed and whole."
I Peter 1:3-5 The Message

WEDNESDAY
THE ALONE ISSUE
I Kings 19:9-18

Not only did God promise never to leave or forsake you in Hebrews 13:5, but you can also be sure you are in good company with other God-followers who are facing battles similar to your own.

The prophet Elijah had his ups and downs. At one point of discouragement, he complained to God *two times in a row*, claiming, "And I alone am left; and they seek my life, to take it away."

If I were God, I might have said to Elijah, "Stop the pity party!" But God dealt gently with his unhappy prophet. The second time Elijah complained, God responded by giving him a clear task, promising him purpose and success, and finally, in I Kings 19:18, lovingly addressing the "alone issue."

> Yet I will leave 7,000 in Israel, all the knees that have not bowed to Baal.

You are not alone today! You have Him and your fellow soldiers.

THURSDAY
ISN'T GOD SOMETHING ELSE?!?
I Kings 21:17-28

There are so many kings listed in the Old Testament, it's nearly impossible to remember them all. Many of us remember Saul, David, and Solomon. Do you remember Ahab, Jezebel's husband? Ahab was the "mother" of all evil kings! Today's passage says, "He sold himself to do evil in the eyes of the Lord." You can't get much worse than that!

Yet you can sense a note of pride in the voice of our God—our wonderful, incredible, forgiving, merciful, amazing God—when He brought Ahab's change of attitude to Elijah's attention.

> "Have you noticed how Ahab has humbled himself before me?"

If you ever have trouble thinking God can't possibly forgive *you*—at least not completely—remember

God's joy when Ahab, the "mother" of all evil, simply humbled himself before Him.

FRIDAY
SUMMARY OF YOUR LIFE
Reading of the Day: I Kings 22:51-53

I Kings 22 gives a summary of the life of King Ahaziah in the last verse of the chapter:

> "He served and worshiped Baal and
> provoked the LORD,
> the God of Israel, to anger, just as
> his father had done."

Little did King Ahaziah know that down through the ages millions of people would read this bleak summary of his life. I am sure it would have blown Ahaziah's mind to think of people reading about him *two millennia* after the Messiah had walked the earth!

There are several kings in the Old Testament who have their lives summarized in one short phrase or statement.

Take a moment to think about what you would want recorded about your own sojourn on earth. Then live today with that in mind!

SATURDAY
HE WAS A LEPER
Reading of the Day: II Chronicles 26:1-4, 16-19, 23

King Uzziah had so much potential! He would have left a great heritage if only the story ended at II Chronicles 26:4: "He did right in the sight of the Lord." But the next verse foreshadows what is to become of him: "As long as he sought the Lord, God prospered him."

Uzziah had many great accomplishments. He reigned 52 years, defeated the Philistines and the Arabs, was famous and powerful, built cities and towers and creative engines of war, dug many cisterns, developed the land, and raised up a powerful army. But he did not continue to seek the Lord. In face of so much success, "his heart was so proud that he acted corruptly and was unfaithful to the Lord his God." (26:16)

Despite all his accomplishments, here is the pitiful summary of his life:

"He was a leper."

Live in faithful obedience every single
"today" God gives you.

SUNDAY
MORE EPITAPHS
Reading of the Day: II Chronicles 19:1-7

On Friday, you read about the summary of King Ahaziah's life:

> "He served and worshiped Baal
> and provoked the LORD,
> the God of Israel, to anger,
> just as his father had done."

In II Chronicles 21:20 the epitaph of King Jehoram is at least as bleak:

> "He passed away, to no one's regret."

I can almost picture these inscriptions on tombstones in a cemetery for kings. Thankfully, if we keep walking down the row, we come across the gravestone for King Jehoshaphat:

> "He sought the Lord with all his heart."
> II Chronicles 22:9 (see also 20:32)

As you can see in today's reading, even Jehoshaphat had his ups and downs. Serious ones! But it's encouraging to know years later he was remembered by the people for his desire to seek God above all else.

> Live today for what might be written
> about you tomorrow!

MONDAY
DEALING FAITHFULLY
Reading of the Day: II Kings 12:9-15

The reign of King Joash teaches valuable lessons about stewardship. The king had directed the priests to collect money and use it to repair the Lord's house. Eventually he discovered that the money wasn't making it any further than the priests' pockets.

When a chest was set up for the people's donations, "All the officers and all the people rejoiced and brought in their levies." (2 Chronicles 24:10) The funds were given directly to the workmen, and no accounting was necessary, *"for they dealt faithfully."* (II Kings 12:16)

We are called to be faithful stewards of our time, energy, health, words, strength, resources, and relationships. As you go through each hour of today, make this your prayer:

This hour is my gift to You

TUESDAY
NOTHING IS IRREDEEMABLE
Reading of the Day: Romans 8:26-28

*In all my prayers, whether I get the answer
I want or not, I can count on one fact:
God can make use of whatever happens.*

Nothing is irredeemable.
—Philip Yancey

Teach me, O God, so to use all the circumstances of my life today that they may bring forth in me the fruits of holiness rather than the fruits of sin.
—John Baillie

The following are also thoughts from John Baillie:

- Let me use disappointment as material for patience.

- Let me use success as material for thankfulness.

- Let me use trouble as material for perseverance.

- Let me use praise as material for humility.

- Let me use pain as material for endurance.

"Devote yourselves to prayer, being watchful and thankful."
Colossians 4:2

WEDNESDAY
AS YOU WISH!
Reading of the Day: Jonah 4:1-11

Sometimes we are a lot like Jonah. We need to recognize God uses us—sometimes when our spirits are willing and at other times when we are unco-operative. Yet, though He chooses to be glorified in and through us, often we are still not pleased.

Jonah first ran away from God's plan. Though he ended up in the belly of a fish, still, "[The sailors] feared the Lord greatly, and they offered a sacrifice to the Lord and made vows." (Jonah 1:16) So even though he was disobeying, God used Jonah!

When Jonah *obeyed* and preached to the Ninevites, "Then the people of Nineveh believed in God." (3:5) God was pleased with the response of the people. So, when Jonah obeyed, God again used him!

> "But it greatly displeased Jonah and
> he became angry." (4:1)

How sad that what pleased God displeased this stubborn, defiant prophet! Pray today:

> *Thank You that you choose to use me Lord.*
> *Let what pleases You, please me!*

THURSDAY
DIVINE APPOINTMENTS
Reading of the Day: Jonah chapter 2

When we think of "divine appointment," rarely do worms, fish, plants, and scorching heat come to mind. But the book of Jonah can open our eyes to the ways God can use just about anything. God certainly appointed Jonah to preach to the people of Nineveh. But He also "appointed a great fish to swallow Jonah." (Jonah 1:17)

I love the words Jonah uttered from the stomach of the fish!

> "I called out of my distress to the Lord,
> and He answered me." *

Consider other divine appointments in the life of Jonah:

- So the Lord appointed a plant.
- But God appointed a worm.
- God appointed a scorching east wind.

Whatever God puts in your path today, don't rule out its divine appointment!

*Note that Jonah prayed this while still in the stomach of the fish. "Called out" and "answered me" are in the *past* tense. "Inside the fish" describes his *present* situation.

FRIDAY
SABER VS. CONOCER
Reading of the Day: Job 42:1-6

Whether Job spoke Spanish or not, he grasped the difference between two Spanish verbs: saber and conocer.

They both mean "to know." But saber is head knowledge. Conocer is to know personally, by experience.

But to *really* know is sort of like my experience at Yosemite National Park. I'd seen all the pictures before visiting the park. But to stand at Glacier Point and gaze in awe at the Half Dome goes far beyond studying the photos and Googling "Yosemite."

Job certainly trusted God when he said, "Though he slay me, yet will I trust in him." But when God spoke to Job and his friends, Job came to a whole new level of understanding of His Maker.

"My ears had heard of you (saber), but now my eyes have seen you (conocer)."
Job 42:5

May you grow in your "conocimiento" of God today!

SATURDAY
BRETHREN VALUES
Reading of the Day: I Corinthians 1:26-2:2

"For I resolved to know nothing while I was with you except Jesus Christ and him crucified."
I Corinthians 2:2

What is Christianity? It is Christ. Nothing more. Nothing less. Christianity is not an ideology or a philosophy... [it is] the good news that beauty, truth, and goodness are found in a person. And true humanity and community are founded on and experienced by connection to that person.

—Leonard Sweet

From my years of fellowship with believers that people refer to as "the brethren," one of the precious values I acquired is the primacy of the Lord Jesus Christ. Whatever may be going on around you, whatever is weighing on your mind, whatever is happening in your life today, be determined

> **"To know nothing except Jesus Christ, and Him crucified."**

SUNDAY
CONFORMABLE OR COMFORTABLE?
Reading of the Day: Galatians 2:15-21

God, help me not to whine!
—Martha Wall, missionary to the lepers of French Niger in the 1940's

In her book, *Splinters from an African Log*, Martha Wall prayed,

> "*[I pray]* that I may know him, and the power of his resurrection, and the fellowship of his sufferings, being made conformable unto his death."
> Philippians 3:10 KJV

How painful it can be to be made conformable unto His death! As Martha Wall suffered through fractures, a serious burn, infection, illnesses, and pain, she wrote, "Had I a choice, I should have fled from this death, renouncing my willingness; but God knew that deep in my heart I still desired His best for me, though I cringed as Jesus never did."

Are you willing today to surrender your "right" to be *comfortable* in order to be made *conformable* unto His death?

Prayer for today: *God, help me not to whine!*

MONDAY
CREATE SPACE FOR GOD
Reading of the Day: Nehemiah 1:4-11

God often speaks to us quietly. He can use memories, phrases from the Bible, an email, or a friend's passing comment. When God speaks, hope is renewed, forgiveness is offered, action is taken on behalf of others, and comfort zones are temporarily left behind.

Henri Nouwen suggested we should "create space in which God can act." It's so easy to fill all the spaces of our lives with commitments and time spent on our newest technology. Like Nehemiah, who mourned and fasted and prayed for several days, make the effort to create space in your life today to listen to God. Time spent waiting on Him is never time wasted.

> *Although I cannot control the sense of*
> *God's presence—on an emotional level,*
> *it will come and go— I can actively wait*
> *for it and attend to it.*
> —Philip Yancey

"Be still and know that I am God."
Psalm 46:10

TUESDAY
THE GREATEST TRAGEDY
Reading of the Day: Matthew 6:5-15

> *The greatest tragedy in life*
> *Is not unanswered prayer,*
> *But unoffered prayer.*
> —F. B. Meyer

I'm intentionally leaving extra space here so you will create a space to listen to God.

Take a few moments to pray.

Right now!

WEDNESDAY
THE GENTLE HEALER
Reading of the Day: Hosea 5:13-6:3

It's sad to hear God's words in Hosea 5:15, "I will go away and return to My place until they acknowledge their guilt and seek My face." But what hope He gives when He continues! "In their affliction they will earnestly seek Me. Come, let us return to the Lord, for He has torn us, but He will heal us; He has wounded us, but He will bandage us."

As a nurse, I really like the thought of God bandaging my wounds. I recently went to a doctor who had a calm, assuring touch. God is that kind of doctor.

Do you have wounds today? Let the Gentle Healer bandage you!

"Let us acknowledge the Lord;
Let us press on to acknowledge Him.
As surely as the sun rises, He will appear."
Hosea 6:3

THURSDAY
HOSEA'S TO-DO LIST
Reading of the Day: Hosea 10:11-15

Sow, Reap, Break, Seek, Plant, Reap, Eat: some of the many verbs in the above passage.

Hosea gives some good suggestions for what you should do and not do today:

Here's your to-do list:
> ***Sow*** for yourselves righteousness,
> ***Reap*** the fruit of unfailing love,
> And ***break up*** your unplowed ground;
> For it is time to ***seek*** the LORD,
> > until he comes and showers righteousness on you.

And **not** to do list:
> But you have ***planted*** wickedness,
> You have ***reaped*** evil,
> You have ***eaten*** the fruit of deception.

FRIDAY
A TENDER FATHER
Reading of the Day: Hosea 11

God spoke to His people through the prophet Hosea, reminding them:

"It was I who taught Ephraim to walk,
taking them by the arms;
but they did not realize it was I who healed them."
Hosea 11:3

Do you remember being taught to walk? Neither do I, and neither did the people of Israel.

Like a loving father tenderly coaxing his child to take his first steps, so God lovingly teaches us to walk in Him. As a mother patiently teaches her child to eat solid food from a spoon, so God desires to teach us to nourish ourselves and find our sufficiency in Him.

Thank Him today for things you seldom recognize your tender, loving Father has done for you.

"I led them with cords of human kindness,
with ties of love;
I lifted the yoke from their neck and
bent down to feed them."
Hosea 11:4

SATURDAY
SLOW AND UNPRODUCTIVE
Reading of the Day: I Peter 4:12-16

If we are faced with difficulties, sometimes prayer seems entirely too slow and unproductive a response.

Yet prayer is the first place we should turn, and time spent on our knees is never unproductive.

When reading the epistles of Peter and Paul, it's important to recognize these letters were often written from prison, while the writer was facing persecution. That makes their advice especially poignant.

Peter preached hope and peace to the dispersed Jews facing extreme persecution, admonishing them, "Cast all your anxiety on Him because He cares for you." I Peter 5:7

Do you ever let anxiety keep you from prayer? Instead, see prayer as a place to deposit your anxiety.

"I have told you these things, so that in me you may have peace.
In this world you will have trouble. But take heart!
I have overcome the world."
The words of Jesus in John 16:33

SUNDAY
GEESE AND SQUIRRELS
Reading of the Day: Romans 10:5-11

So what in the world does Romans 10 have to do with geese and squirrels? I'll do my best to tie the two together. Have you ever heard of the sayings, "He ain't got the brains that God gave squirrels?"

or "She ain't got the sense that God gave geese?" Sometimes the animals do better at giving glory to God than we humans do!

T. McIlwain wrote, "God gave man a mind, emotions, and a will so that man could know, love, and obey God.... Animals are not able to know, love, and obey God like man can."

Isaiah 1:3 is the Biblical version of the sayings above about geese and squirrels:

> "An ox knows its owner, and a donkey
> its master's manger,
> but Israel does not know, my people
> do not understand."

Live up to your potential today by
- Recognizing your Owner

- Loving your Lord

- Obeying your Master's voice

MONDAY
FAITH IN THE FACE OF FEAR
Reading of the Day: Nehemiah 4:7-15

Are you facing anything today that causes you fear? Life dishes up plenty of reasons to fear. The remnant in Jerusalem at the time of Nehemiah had plenty of troubles. They faced credible threats and opposition, so the swords strapped to their sides 24/7 were totally necessary. The people were continually at risk of their work and their very lives being destroyed.

Nehemiah responded in faith and in prayer, and led his people to follow suit:

"But we prayed to our God, and because of them we set up a guard against them day and night."

In verse 14 we read,

"When I saw [the people's] fear, I rose and spoke… 'Do not be afraid of them; **Remember the Lord who is great and awesome.'**"

Remember today, in the face of fear, you have a God who is great and awesome. Turn to Him in prayer, and then step out in faith!

TUESDAY
RECOLLECT YOURSELF
Reading of the Day: Isaiah 55:6-11

"Seek the Lord while He may be found;
Call on Him while He is near."
Isaiah 55:6

Let us become accustomed to recollect ourselves, during the day and in the course of our duties, by a single look toward God. Let us thus quiet all the movement of our hearts, as soon as we see them agitated. Let us separate ourselves from all pleasure which does not come from God. Let us cut off futile thoughts and dreams. Let us not speak empty words. Let us seek God… and we shall find him without fail.

—François Fénelon

What is shorter than a "breath prayer"? Just a single look toward God! Be intentional today, and set an alarm to remind you later to "look toward God."

WEDNESDAY
ONCE-IN-A-LIFETME
OPPORTUNITY
Reading of the Day: Psalm 50:7-15

"He who sacrifices thank offerings honors me."
Psalm 50:23

Our reactions to everyday occurrences can change a piece of history and bring glory to God. There are many things that can glorify the Living God, the Creator of the Universe. We might think honoring God in this life would require painting the greatest painting, preaching to thousands, writing a symphony, or caring for the poor. Certainly, those all would bring glory to God. But today you have a unique opportunity to honor Him. If you respond with a sacrifice of thank offerings, whatever life hands you today, you are honoring Him!

You'll have many once-in-a-lifetime opportunities today to glorify Him. Take advantage of those moments!

THURSDAY
HAVE MERCY ON ME!
Reading of the Day: Luke 18:9-14

"God, have mercy on me, a sinner!"
Luke 18:13

Do you long to learn to pray continuously? There are many ways to think about and put in practice an attitude of constant prayer. One way of praying continuously is to consciously center all your thoughts and activities around Him, including Him in all you think and do.

Another practice of continuous prayer recently impacted me. I read of a woman who prayed throughout her day, "Lord, have mercy on me!" I decided one day to make that my "breath prayer of the day." That day as I elbowed my way through a noisy group of tourists in a hallway, I stopped in my tracks and said to myself, "Now, Susan! That was not very Christ-like!" Immediately I was reminded of my call to prayer, "God, have mercy on me!" That prayer gave way to a new compassion for the people I had just elbowed my way through. I added a PS prayer, "God have mercy on *them*, too!"

Remember these two short prayers throughout your day:

God have mercy on me! God have mercy on them, too!

FRIDAY
A GOD-PHRASE
Reading of the Day: I Kings 19:9-18

If prayer means conversation with God, then God must speak as well, or else it would be simply a monologue. Yesterday I asked you to pray a short prayer throughout the day. Today I challenge you to think of a phrase that **God speaks to you** instead of simply you speaking to God. Let me explain by giving you an example from the life of Amy Carmichael, a missionary to India in the early 20th century. As she was riding on a train one day, listening to the clickety-clack of the wheels on the rails, she heard repeatedly the voice of God saying to her,

"Let it be. Think of Me. Let it be. Think of Me." As humans, we tend to hold onto things that God would have us let go of… for instance, resentments, possessions, and negative thoughts. Our minds can get wrapped up in all the things we so desperately need to leave behind.

Pause to ask God if there is anything He is saying to you right now. Either repeat your own God-phrase throughout your day, or remind yourself of,

"Let it be. Think of Me."

SATURDAY
ENEMIES
Reading of the Day: Matthew 5:43-48

"But I tell you: 'Love your enemies and pray for those who persecute you.'"
Matthew 5:44

No one needs our love more than the unlovely. We should stand beside our enemies and plead to God on their behalf. After all, who else will pray for them?

I can't honestly say I have many enemies. But, while in Rome with friends a few years ago, I was convicted to pray for someone who had wronged me. Two of us were robbed by a band of thieves... a group of young moms carrying babies! We caught one of the women and actually ended up spending over an hour with her in a small, hot, smoky office, filing a police report. Thanks to my husband Woody's thoughtful prompt, I shared a chocolate bar with the woman who'd just stolen from us. That Kit Kat bar reminded me to love her and to pray for her and her small child.

SUNDAY
LOOK TO HIM
Reading of the Day: Psalm 123

"As the eyes of slaves look to the
hand of their master,
As the eyes of a female slave look to the
hand of her mistress,
So our eyes look to the LORD our God,
till he shows us his mercy."
Psalm 123:2

MY VERSION:
As the eyes of Celeste used to look to me,
So may my eyes look to You, O Lord my God, until
You show me Your mercy!

While living in Costa Rica, Woody used to sit at
the bottom of our steps in the evening, letting our
Great Dane, Celeste, put her huge paws on his
shoulders as he would pet her. She obviously was
in "dog heaven" with Woody's TLC, but her neck
was craning and her eyes were still always looking
around for me. Remember that word picture today,
and look to Him!

MONDAY
MAKE YOUR LIFE A PRAYER
Reading of the Day: Colossians 4:2-6

"Devote yourselves to prayer,
being watchful and thankful…
Be wise in the way you act toward outsiders; make
the most of every opportunity."
Colossians 4:2, 5

One of the many things I learned from my mentor, Win, was to include God as part of my conversations with people. I don't mean to just talk *about* God, but to actually *include* Him as part of our conversation. When Win and I talked together, she often spontaneously directed her conversation to God, asking Him to have her words be His Words or thanking Him for some element of our friendship.

Think of your conversations with people today as communication which includes God. Talk to Jesus, asking Him to turn your lunch or coffee break into a prayer.

Don't just read a chapter from the Bible. Pray it! When you willingly turn your activities towards God, intentionally including Him and speaking with Him, your life becomes a prayer.

TUESDAY
MENTAL MONOLOGUE V.
DIVINE DIALOGUE
Reading of the Day: Psalm 150

"Let every thing that hath breath praise the Lord."
Psalm 150:6 KJV

Do you ever talk to yourself? According to a survey I read recently, most people do, so don't worry! Lately I've begun to wonder if God actually created us that way—not in order to talk to ourselves, but to turn our self-talk to Him.

The key to praying continually is to transform our continual inner dialogue into a communication with God. Instead of fretting to yourself, "What am I going to do *now?*" try praying sincerely, "Lord, what should I do now?" Instead of thinking, "Man, I just can't do this anymore!" Pray, "God, in my own strength I cannot continue. Thank You that I can claim the promise that I can do all things through Christ who gives me strength."

Naturally, our inner dialogue tends toward self-centeredness.

Intentionally turn your focus to God.
Turn your mental monologue into a divine dialogue!

WEDNESDAY
UNLIMITED POSSIBILITIES
Reading of the Day: II Corinthians 5:1-10

The following thoughts from Edith Schaeffer's book, *Affliction*, have deeply impacted my life.

"Our reactions, and what we actively do as a result of them, cannot only change a piece of history but can bring glory to God. We are meant never to forget—no matter how shrill the wind, how violent the storm—that there is meaning and purpose in our lives. There is unlimited possibility for glorifying God—moment by moment, hour by hour, every day in every situation. How? By offering praise, not with our lips and throats in repetitive cadence, saying the words while our minds and emotions are filled with other thoughts and feelings, but by actually loving and trusting God when there is pressure being brought upon us to not trust Him."

Don't measure your spiritual value by what great things you might accomplish for God. Measure it by your trust in Him in all things today.

THURSDAY
WAITING ON OUR COMFORT
Reading of the Day: Isaiah 45:1-6

Thomas á Kempis wrote,

"My Lord Jesus, do not be far from me, but come quickly and help me, for I am terrified by fears of the future. How shall I break their power over me? How shall I go unhurt without your help? O Lord, You have promised, 'I myself will prepare your way, leveling mountains and hills. I will open the gates of the prison, and reveal to you the hidden treasures of spiritual knowledge.'"

"O Lord, do as you have said, drive away all my fears. This is my hope and my only comfort - to turn to you, to put all my trust in you, to call inwardly upon you, and to wait for your comfort with patience."

What a calling—to wait on Him for our comfort with patience!

FRIDAY
WRITE YOUR OWN VERSION
Reading of the Day: Habakkuk 3:14-19

I am fascinated with the prophet Habakkuk and the book which records his struggles with God. Strife, oppression, and wickedness were rampant in Judah at the time, yet God seemingly did nothing. When God finally said He would act, He promised to do so through the wicked Babylonians. To have God choose to work through such a godless people only added to the prophet's confusion. It is so moving to walk through the emotions and thoughts expressed by Habakkuk and then join him in the conclusion,

> "Though the fig tree does not bud and
> there are no grapes on the vines,
> though the olive crop fails and
> the fields produce no food,
> though there are no sheep in the
> pen and no cattle in the stalls,
> yet I will rejoice in the LORD,
> I will be joyful in God my Savior.
> The Sovereign LORD is my strength;
> he makes my feet like the feet of a deer,
> he enables me to go on the heights."
> Habakkuk 3:17-19

Take a moment to fit your own circumstances into the above passage as a personalized prayer. Be creative!

SATURDAY
WHO'S A FOOL?
Reading of the Day: Jeremiah 37:1-8

"Neither he nor his attendants nor the people of
the land *paid any attention*
to the words the LORD had spoken
through Jeremiah the prophet.
King Zedekiah, however, sent a
message to Jeremiah requesting,
'Please pray to the LORD our God for us.'"
Jeremiah 37:2-3

King Zedekiah was unwilling to pay attention to
God's words spoken through Jeremiah. So why in
the world did he send messengers to the prophet to
ask him to pray?

Before you are quick to write this king off as a fool,
think about your own life. Are there ways you are
unwilling to listen to God's Word? Take two steps
right now: 1) Pray that God will give you willingness to listen and obey, and 2) Ask someone to pray
for you, that you would be sensitive to God's voice
and willing to obey.

SUNDAY
REVERSE ROLE MODELS
Reading of the Day: II Chronicles 36:11-14

As a child of God, train yourself to use everything in life as a stimulus to pray. For instance, when reading the Scripture, learn to observe qualities of the lives of Biblical characters, and turn those into a prayer, asking Him to help you reflect His character and priorities in your life.

We can learn from the lives of those who *displeased* God as well as from the example of His humble, obedient servants.

"[Zedekiah] did evil in the eyes of the LORD his God and did not humble himself before Jeremiah the prophet, who spoke the word of the LORD…
He became stiff-necked and hardened his heart and would not turn to the LORD,
the God of Israel."
II Chronicles 36:11-13

Use the phrases from the above passage to turn this evil king's life into your own prayer:

- May I do good in Your eyes
- May I humble myself before You

- May I not have a stiff neck
- May I not have a hard heart

MONDAY
HAVE THINE OWN WAY
Reading of the Day: Jeremiah 18:1-12

Romans 9:20-21 comes across pretty bluntly in the New Living Translation:

> "Who are you, a mere human being,
> to argue with God?
> Should the thing that was created
> say to the one who created it,
> 'Why have you made me like this?'
> When a potter makes jars out of clay, doesn't he
> have a right to use the same lump of clay
> to make one jar for decoration and another to
> throw garbage into?"

In the early 1900's, Adelaide Pollard wanted to serve as a missionary in Africa, but was unable to raise the necessary funds for the trip. One night she heard a woman pray, "It really doesn't matter what You do with us, Lord, just have your way in our lives." When Pollard returned to her room that night, she spent time meditating on Jeremiah 18:3,4: "So I went down to the potter's house, and I saw him working at the wheel. But the pot he was shaping from the clay was marred in his hands; so the potter formed it into another pot, shaping it as seemed best to him."

Adelaide then penned these well-known words:

Have Thine own way, Lord! Have Thine own way!
Wounded and weary, help me, I pray!
Power, all power, surely is Thine!
Touch me and heal me, Savior divine!

TUESDAY
180° PRAYER
Reading of the Day: Zephaniah 3:1-5

Someday I'd like to write a book called *180° Prayers*, taking Biblical admonitions and turning them around into prayers.

The other day we looked at King Zedekiah's bad example and turned it into a prayer. Read below Zephaniah's prophecy from chapter 3, verse 2 about Jerusalem's moral decay.

"She obeys no one, she accepts no correction.
She does not trust in the LORD, she does not
draw near to her God."

Take a moment to make this verse take a 180° turn and become your own prayer. I'll give you my personal example here to get your own creative juices flowing.

Lord, I declare my trust in You, though I feel like I'm wading through a muddy life swamp right now. I want to draw near to You, but I feel like I can't even take that first step without Your tug. There's no way to budge without You! But I don't want to stay stuck. I want to listen, whether it be You speaking to me through Your Word or even through the painful observations of others. Give me the will and the way to listen to You and obey.

WEDNESDAY
LIFE BEYOND SELF
Reading of the Day: Zephaniah 2:13-15

"I am, and there is no one besides me."
Zephaniah 2:15

You might think this Scripture is quoting God's words about Himself. Sadly, it is not. Many people over the ages have committed "The Babylonian Error" of declaring, "I am, and there is no one besides me." It's likely we commit that same error more often than we'd dare admit! We may not say those exact words, but our attitudes and behavior shout this selfish refrain. We are prone to selfishness. We are prone to stealing God's place at the center of the universe.

Give God His proper place today. Confess aloud,

"You are! And there is none besides You!"

Write that phrase out, and put it somewhere as a reminder throughout your day. Recognize your place as the pot on the Potter's wheel.

THURSDAY
GOD IS OUR SANCTUARY
Ezekiel 11:12-20

Even though the Israelites were in captivity in Babylon, suffering justly for their unfaithfulness, God says of them,

"Yet I was a sanctuary for them a little while in the countries where they had gone."
Ezekiel 11:16

Do you find yourself in need of a sanctuary today?
Do you seek refuge?
Do you need peace?

Whether your needs result from your own wrong choices or simply because life never ceases to present challenges, remember:

He is your sanctuary of refuge and peace today.

FRIDAY
IN ONE SPOT OR ANOTHER
Reading of the Day: Hebrews 10:32-39

It is likely today you will find yourself in one of two spots described in Hebrews 10:32-33:

"Remember those earlier days … sometimes you were publicly exposed to insult and persecution; at other times you stood side by side with those who were so treated."

We find ourselves either exposed to insult and persecution or standing by others who are so treated. Standing close to someone who is hurting hurts! God knows. He does it every day. His grace is not only sufficient for those who are hurting, but for those standing by their side.

If you don't find yourself in either category today, take a moment right now to pray for believers who are facing difficulties or persecution. Stand in the gap for them!

SATURDAY
DECLARATION OF COMMITMENT, DAY 1
Reading of the Day: Esther 4: 9-16

I have broken down a declaration of commitment to read over the next four days. The Scripture readings for each of the four days present different Biblical examples and teaching about courageously stepping up to God's calling.

Saddleback Church's Angel Stadium Declaration
By Pastor Rick Warren, April 14, 2005

Today I am stepping across the line. I'm tired of waffling, and I'm finished with wavering. I've made my choice; the verdict is in; and my decision is irrevocable. I'm going God's way. There's no turning back now!

I will live the rest of my life serving God's purposes with God's people on God's planet for God's glory. I will use my life to celebrate his presence, cultivate his character, participate in his family, demonstrate his love, and communicate his Word.

SUNDAY
DECLARATION OF COMMITMENT, DAY 2
Reading of the Day: Joshua 1:1-9

Joshua was a man who had the unusual experience of being called to action by the Lord Himself speaking directly to him. Make the next segment of the Angel Stadium Declaration into your own heart's cry:

Since my past has been forgiven, and I have a purpose for living and a home awaiting in heaven, I refuse to waste any more time or energy on shallow living, petty thinking, trivial talking, thoughtless doing, useless regretting, hurtful resenting, or faithless worrying. Instead I will magnify God, grow to maturity, serve in ministry, and fulfill my mission in the membership of his family.

Because this life is preparation for the next, I will value worship over wealth, "we" over "me," character over comfort, service over status, and people over possessions, position, and pleasures. I know what matters most, and I'll give it all I've got. I'll do the best I can with what I have for Jesus Christ today.

MONDAY
DECLARATION OF COMMITMENT, DAY 3
Reading of the Day: Isaiah 43:1-7

I have sat through many commencement addresses where the intent was to motivate the graduates to go forward and change their world. Glancing around the crowd of new graduates and their friends and families, I noted I was certainly not the only one bored, thinking, "When can I get out of here?"

As we've been looking at the challenge led by Rick Warren and the stories of men and women in the Bible who stepped up to risk their lives as they were called by God, I have been most impressed by the words of God Himself. In very few words, He can have the crowds trembling either in fear of judgment or enraptured by a glorious hope of the future. Isaiah 43 is one of those "divine commencement addresses" that would never find the graduates nodding off. Here's the third day of our four-day series, calling us to commitment:

I won't be captivated by culture, manipulated by critics, motivated by praise, frustrated by problems, debilitated by temptation, or intimidated by the devil. I'll keep running my race with my eyes on the goal, not the sidelines or those running by me. When times get tough, and I get tired, I won't back up, back off, back down, back out, or backslide. I'll just keep moving forward by God's grace. I'm Spirit-led, purpose-driven and mission-focused, so I cannot be bought, I will not be compromised, and I shall not quit until I finish the race.

TUESDAY
DECLARATION OF COMMITMENT, DAY 4
Reading of the Day: Revelation 2:8-11

Reading through the book of Revelation cannot help but stimulate us to new levels of commitment. The messages to the seven churches in the first chapters promise suffering and persecution, but at the same time offer hope of eternal reward to those who remain faithful to the end.

I'm a trophy of God's amazing grace, so I will be gracious to everyone, grateful for every day, and generous with everything that God entrusts to me.

To my Lord and Savior Jesus Christ, I say: However, whenever, wherever, and whatever you ask me to do, my answer in advance is yes! Wherever you lead and whatever the cost, I'm ready.

Anytime. Anywhere. Any way.

Whatever it takes Lord; whatever it takes! I want to be used by you in such a way, that on that final day I'll hear you say,

"Well done, thou good and faithful one. Come on in, and let the eternal party begin!"

The party is about to begin, so put on the special clothes provided by the host, join the everlasting throng, and crown Him Lord of all!

WEDNESDAY
CARKING CARE
Reading of the Day: Psalm 139:1-6, 17-18, 23-24

"Search me, O God, and know my heart;
test me and know my anxious thoughts.
See if there is any offensive way in me,
And lead me in the way everlasting."
Psalm 139:23-24

Recently I have been reading a collection of Puritan prayers in *The Valley of Vision*. There are some phrases in there that intrigue me that I've included in the following prayer.

Lord, when I am feeling the weight of cares upon me; when I am perplexed and don't know what to do, help me, I pray. If you see in my heart any nest of sin, then grant me the kiss of Your forgiveness. Deliver me from carking* care and help me to follow Christ with a firm and brave step today; through His power wrestling successfully against weakness. Make me a perfume of praiseful gratitude to You.

*Causing distress or worry.

THURSDAY
ASK AND THINK. THINK AND ASK.
Reading of the Day: Ephesians 3:14-21

"Now to Him who is able to do far more abundantly beyond all that we ask or think."
Ephesians 4:20

I have been trying to become more aware of what I am thinking during the day. Each time I pause briefly to consider that, I challenge myself to turn those thoughts into a prayer.

Ephesians 4:20 says God can do more than we ask

or think. Today my challenge for you is "think and ask." Set your phone alarm or create another kind of reminder so that throughout your day you pause to consider what you are thinking and turn that into a prayer.

For example, right now I am thinking, "Will this entry be good enough to include in my manuscript? How many more entries do I need to write?" That can readily be turned into the following prayer:

Lord, may every single entry read in this book be used in Your hands as a tool of Your Holy Spirit. Give me Your energy and wisdom as I finish my writing and editing, and powerfully bless the person reading this right now!

FRIDAY
GOD'S PURPOSES
Reading of the Day: John 21:15-17

I am pleased to include the following entry from my daughter, Norma Porter. She has been a missionary for many years with her family in Cochabamba, Bolivia. Here are her words:

Several years ago, I went through a time of depression because of some things that were happening in my life. During that time, I learned that God is a God of opportunities and He never lets me go, even when I've failed Him… and know I will fail Him again.

Jesus declared to Peter in Matthew 16:18, "And I tell you that you are Peter, and on this rock I will build my church." He knew that this same Peter would deny Him three times at His time of greatest need. Yet, he chose very man to build His church.

If we repent and we return to God, He forgives us and continues to choose us to showcase His glory. Let the life of Peter remind you:

> Your past sins do not void
> God's purposes in your life.

SATURDAY
DID, STILL, AND WILL
Reading of the Day: II Corinthians 1:3-11

Man's extremity is often God's opportunity. Take a moment to meditate on my paraphrase of II Corinthians 1:10:

> "We were completely overwhelmed,
> but we believe we felt this way so we
> might learn to trust,
> not in ourselves, but in the powerful
> God of Resurrection.

He is the One who *did* preserve us,
still is preserving us,
and *will* preserve us because
we put our full trust in Him."

Is there some way you are feeling overwhelmed today? Or do you know of someone who is feeling overwhelmed? Remind yourself (or encourage someone else through a phone call or in the course of your conversations today) of:

- God's faithfulness in the past,

- His presence in the present, and

- His promise for the future.

SUNDAY
PLEASE LEAVE!
Reading of the Day: Mark 5:11-20

"Please leave! ... Let me go with you!"
Mark 5:17-18 (my paraphrase)

You can't have it both ways. It's either "Please leave!" or "Let me go with You!" Mark chapter 5 gives the dramatic account of a demon-possessed man. When Jesus drove "Legion" into the herd of pigs, they rushed down the steep bank into the sea. The people were so frightened by the events they implored Jesus, "Please leave!"

But a dramatic change had taken place, and this drama didn't have to do with the pigs. The man who had been demon-possessed was now "clothed and in his right mind... [He] was imploring Jesus that he might accompany Him."

I'm sure you would not intentionally ask Jesus to "please leave." It's quite possible, however, that in some areas of your life you would prefer Jesus would "please leave" well enough alone! Do a quick attitude check (see if you are in your "right mind"), and make sure your heart's desire is to accompany Jesus today.

MONDAY
SMELL THE ROSES!
Reading of the Day: John 1:1-14

"Though the world was made through Him, the world did not recognize Him."
John 1:10b

When I lived in Costa Rica, every morning I would take time to weed our garden. I recently read about someone who had a similar routine. When his wife accompanied him one day, she marveled at the beautiful wildflowers surrounding them. He looked up, amazed. Every day he had been so focused on the weeds, he had not even noticed the flowers! Sadly, I am often guilty of the same practice.

Take time today to smell the roses. Think about an area of your life in which you have been focusing on the weeds. Look for the opportunities to see the grain of good and to offer praise and thanksgiving. Don't overlook the work of God all around you.

TUESDAY
DIVINE INTERRUPTIONS
Reading of the Day: Matthew 14:22-33

"After He had sent the crowds away, He went up on the mountain by Himself to pray."
Matthew 14:23

If you don't intentionally reserve moments for prayer, don't count on those times happening on their own account. Jesus Himself had to send the needy crowds away in order to be by Himself to pray.

When you pray each morning, bring to God every planned conversation and commitment. Ask Him to keep your eyes open to divine interruptions. When you humbly preview your day in prayer, He will rearrange your priorities throughout the course of the day.

As you pray at the day's end, you can review what has happened, reflect on what you have learned, repent of your failings and sins, and give Him all that remains unresolved from your day.

WEDNESDAY
PROPHETIC 180
Reading of the Day: Matthew 13:11-17

Jesus quoted the prophet Isaiah while explaining to His disciples why He spoke to the people in parables. Allow me to turn this passage into a "Prophetic 180 Prayer," using just two verses which Jesus quoted from Isaiah 6:9-10. This "Prophetic 180 Prayer" turns a prophecy of judgment 180°, transforming it into a prayer of repentance or commitment.

> "May I not only keep on hearing, but understand.
> May I not only keep on seeing, but perceive.
> May my ear not become dull, but hear You clearly.
> May I keep my eyes wide open and see You plainly.
> May I hear with my ears and understand with my heart and return,
> and You will heal me."
> Matthew 13:14-15

THURSDAY
ME, POTTER! YOU, CLAY!
Reading of the Day: Isaiah 29:13-16

> "You turn things upside down, as if the potter were thought to be like the clay!
> Shall what is formed say to Him who formed it,
> 'He did not make me'?

Can the pot say of the potter, 'He knows nothing'?"
Isaiah 29:16

Here's what God is saying to you:
>   Me, parent! You, child!
>   Me, God! You, human!
>   Me, Creator! You, creature!
>   Me, Potter! You, clay!

Take a moment to think about areas in your life where you may have gotten your role mixed up.

FRIDAY
SOAKING-WET SANDALS
Reading of the Day: Mark 4:35-41

Often, I try to put myself in others' shoes while reading the Bible. In Matthew 8, the disciples followed Jesus in the boat. Fresh in their minds were the centurion's faith, the healing of Peter's mother-in-law, and the casting out of demons. When a storm arose, the Master was asleep. They awoke Him in a panic, crying, "Lord, save us! We're going to drown!" After He calmed the sea, He said to them, "Do you still have no faith?"

That particular question gives me pause. Think about it for a minute. What if Jesus asked *you* that question? How would you reply, remembering that He knows your heart?

What kind of faith did Jesus expect from His disciples as He slept and the weather turned from bad to life-threatening? What would have pleased Him? If I were in their soaking-wet sandals, could I have responded to the impending disaster any better than they? I think Jesus would have been happy if they'd cried out instead, "Save us! We know You can!"

SATURDAY
THE MASTER CHIROPRACTOR
Reading of the Day: Nehemiah 12:27-43

Take a moment to sing (aloud, if circumstances allow!) this hymn:

> When upon life's billows you are tempest-tossed,
> When you are discouraged, thinking all is lost,
> Count your many blessings; name them one by one,
> And it will surprise you what the Lord hath done.

In today's Scripture reading, Nehemiah assigned two choirs to lead the people in giving thanks. I would have loved to be part of that celebration!

Thirty-three times the words "give thanks" are recorded in God's Word. God knows we need frequent reminders. He longs to hear us give thanks to Him.

Sometimes we find it nearly impossible to have a thankful heart. There is a Master Chiropractor that always knows how to make the perfect adjustments, aligning your attitudes, and enabling you to give thanks. Surrender to Him your bad attitudes, pity parties, and "good reasons" for your complaints. And give thanks in all circumstances you face today.

"Let the peace of Christ rule in your hearts, since
as members of one body
you were called to peace. And be thankful."
Colossians 3:15

SUNDAY
LISTEN UP!
Reading of the Day: Mark 4:21-25

In Mark 4:23-25, we see a promise repeated four times and then turned around and repeated as a warning. (See bold type below.) If Jesus repeats what He is saying, we should pay close attention to it.

"Anyone with ears to hear should listen and **understand**… Pay close attention to what you hear. The closer you listen, the **more understanding** you will be given—and you will receive even more. To those who listen to my teaching, **more understanding** will be given. But for those who are not listening,

even what little **understanding** they have will be
taken away from them."

Mark 4:22-25 NLT

Make this your prayer today:

Help me listen closely and apply what I hear from You.
Help me pay close attention to You.
Increase my understanding, just as You promised!

MONDAY
LEAVING EVERYTHING
Reading of the Day: Matthew 19:21-29

After the rich young man walked away, saddened
by Jesus' command to go and sell all his possessions
to the poor, it occurred to the disciples they had
done exactly what Jesus told the young man to do.

"We have left everything to follow You!
What then will there be for us?"
Matthew 19:27

I can almost sense their excitement about what they
will receive. Though I can't be sure of the motive
behind their question, Jesus' answer did not disap-
point them.

"And everyone who has left houses or brothers or
sisters or father or mother or children or farms for

My name's sake, will receive many times as much,
and will inherit eternal life."
Matthew 19:29

Take a moment today to pray for the Latinos we
have been privileged to mobilize to countries where
their sacrifice is great. They have left much behind
in order to follow Jesus and make Him known in
tough spots in the world.

TUESDAY
CONVENIENT OVERSIGHT
Reading of the Day: Matthew 20:20-28

Considering yesterday's thoughts about what the
disciples had given up, it's interesting to note in the
very next chapter that,

"Then the wife of Zebedee came to
Jesus with her sons.
She bowed before him and asked him to
do something for her."
Matthew 20:20 NCV

I can almost picture James and John excitedly telling their mom about the rich young ruler and
Jesus' delightful promise of reward for his disciples.
I wonder if they forgot to tell her the conclusion
of Jesus' response to the disciples' question, "What
then will there be for us?"

"And everyone who has left houses or brothers or sisters or father or mother or children or farms for My name's sake, will receive many times as much, and will inherit eternal life.

But many who are first will be last; and the last, first."

You can almost see it coming when she asks Jesus to set her boys at His right and left hand in the kingdom.

"You do not know what you are asking…"

It makes me wonder, what parts of Jesus' teaching am *I* conveniently overlooking?

WEDNESDAY
MORE LIKE MOSES
Reading of the Day: Numbers 12:1-9

There are so many character traits we seldom hear about. One is humility. God Himself said of Moses in Numbers 12:3:

"Now Moses was a very humble man, more humble than anyone else on the face of the earth."

When two men in the camp began to prophesy, Joshua told Moses to restrain them. But Moses instead rejoiced that God would bestow His Spirit on others. What an example!

In contrast, Aaron and Miriam proudly cried out,

> "Has the Lord only spoken through Moses?...
> Has He not spoken through us as well?"

Woody often tells stories of being called in to the principal's office when he was in grade school. What if instead of being called to the principal's office, *God himself* called you to the *tabernacle* to reprimand you for speaking and thinking as Aaron and Miriam had?

Ask God to help you be more like Moses today.

THURSDAY
SEE THE POTENTIAL
Reading of the Day: Numbers 14:1-12

A few months ago, I wrote about thinking on whatever is true. The Israelites sure had difficulty doing that! In Numbers 14, they began to weep and wail because of the report the spies brought back from the land of Canaan. Instead of seeing the potential (as God promised!), they visualized, "Our wives and our little ones will become plunder!" They just *knew* that it would have been better to stay in Egypt.

The Israelites were convinced of a grim future reality, even though God promised otherwise. How often do we do the same? We visualize (possibly even based on facts, much like the Israelites) what might happen, and our souls agonize with the prospect.

Focus today instead on God's promises. Joshua and Caleb have a word for you today.

"The Lord is with us; do not be afraid of them."
Numbers 14:9b

FRIDAY
ANOTHER 180° PRAYER
Reading of the Day: Luke 18:9-14

Right before the account of the Pharisee and tax collector praying in the temple, Luke tells the reason for Jesus' parable:

"And He also told this parable to some people who trusted in themselves that they were righteous, and viewed others with contempt."

Give this passage a 180° turn, and make it into your prayer today:

May I trust in You, not in myself today.
May I find my righteousness in You, not in myself.
May I view others through Your eyes.

SATURDAY
NEITHER HOT NOR COLD
Reading of the Day: Revelation 3:14-22

When I worked as a coronary care nurse, we usually were able to tell exactly what people's temperatures were, because we measured the "core temp," the temperature of the blood near the heart. Now *that* is an accurate temperature!

> "So because you are lukewarm—neither hot nor cold—I am about to spit you out of my mouth."
> Revelation 3:16

There is a spiritual application in measuring an accurate temperature. Axillary temps aren't too accurate. (We cannot rightly judge ourselves by the service we perform.) Oral temperatures aren't much better. (Nor can you judge a person only by his words.) Otic (ear) temps are popular, but can you base spirituality on what teachings or music one listens to? God judges rightly by the **core temp**—straight from the heart!

SUNDAY
WHAT IS YOUR PASSION?
Reading of the Day: II Timothy 2:1-10

What are you passionate about? One Sunday I was approached by a church friend who could not stop talking about the potential of ozone water to change my life. That same morning another woman cornered me to talk about what transformed her own life—drinking raw potato juice every morning! As I tried to tactfully escape these diatribes, I began to wonder, "What am I passionate about? If we talk about ozone water and potato juice at church, what do we talk about the rest of the week? Is Jesus really the One I want to talk about?"

"Therefore I endure everything for the sake of the elect, that they too may obtain the salvation that is in Christ Jesus, with eternal glory."
II Timothy 2:10

MONDAY
BLESSED IRONY
Reading of the Day: I Corinthians 9:19-23

A Christian man is the most free lord of all,
and subject to none;
a Christian man is the most dutiful servant of all,
and subject to every one.
—Martin Luther

"Though I am free and belong to no man,
I make myself a slave to
everyone, to win as many as possible."
I Corinthians 9:19

Don't you just love the irony found in the truths of the Word? Just reading through the Old Testament law is exhausting. Imagine trying to know all the laws and keep them! Christ is the fulfillment of the law for us. Rejoice today in the freedom you have in Christ!

Yet, truly one of our highest privileges is to be a servant of the Most Holy God and also a servant of our fellow men.

TUESDAY
FINISH STRONG!
Reading of the Day: I Kings 8:22-30

When Solomon completed the building of the Temple, he gave a moving speech at the dedication ceremony.

"Incline my heart to You, that I may walk in all Your ways… let my heart be fully committed to You, my Lord and God, to walk in Your statutes and keep Your commands."

Solomon started out so well, honoring God by requesting wisdom above all else. God honored him by granting him that wisdom. Solomon honored God in the building and dedication of the Temple. So where did he go wrong?

I wonder if one day he stopped praying the prayer above, or the words became so familiar he began praying it automatically without thinking about its deep meaning. Perhaps once he got to that point, he gradually drifted away from the God who granted him such wisdom.

Keeping in mind Solomon's grave error as he grew old, let's strive to finish strong. Don't let one day pass without making the gist of Solomon's prayer your own heart's cry.

> "Incline my heart to You,
> that I may walk in all Your ways."
> (various Scriptures repeat this same concept.
> See I Kings 8:58, Psalm 119:4-5)

WEDNESDAY
PITCH YOUR TENT
Reading of the Day: Genesis 12:1-7

We are not fugitives running away, nor vagabonds running around, but pilgrims.

As pilgrims, we must pitch our tent and build our altar,
Not pitch our altar and build our tent.
—Betty McGehee, Ladies Retreat, Sandy Creek
Bible Camp 1990

I wrote these comments in the back of an old Bible.

Don't you just love it when you come across old gems that bring back fond memories?

"By faith Abraham… made his home in the promised land like a stranger in a foreign country;
he lived in tents, as did Isaac and Jacob, who were
heirs with him of the same promise.
For he was looking forward to the city with foun-
dations, whose architect and builder is God."
Hebrews 11:8-10

THURSDAY
ONE-EYED DISGRACE
Reading of the Day: I Samuel 11:1-11

In I Samuel there's an obscure story from the short glory days of King Saul. The people of Gad and Reuben had been oppressed for years by the Ammonite king. He had gouged out the right eye of each of the Israelites living in his land. The Ammonite king then made his move against the 7000 men who had escaped to Jabesh Gilead. They begged the king for a treaty and were promised peace at a price. All must lose their right eye "as a disgrace to all Israel." The elders of Jabesh begged, "Give us seven days—if no one comes to save us, we will agree to your terms."

No one had come to their rescue up to this point. Why would they now finally step up to the plate and save their brothers? The story comes to a triumphant finish for Saul and God's people. First, the Spirit of God came upon Saul in power. Second, after Saul called on the people to fight, the "terror of the Lord fell on the people, and they turned out as one man." That very night, by the power of God, the Ammonites were slaughtered.

Consider today how you can offer hope and a future to those whose cries have gone unheard.

FRIDAY
GODLY TREMBLING
Reading of the Day: Isaiah 66:1-6

"The LORD reigns,
let the nations tremble;
he sits enthroned between the cherubim,
let the earth shake." Psalm 99:1

If you know the melody, find a moment and place to softly sing the words of the following song:

Were you there when they crucified my Lord?
Were you there when they crucified my Lord?
Oh! Sometimes it causes me to
tremble, tremble, tremble.
Were you there when they crucified my Lord?

Make this your prayer today:

May I tremble as I read and meditate on Your Word.

What causes you to tremble? God gives good reason to tremble in Isaiah 66:2:

> "These are the ones I look on with favor:
> those who are humble and contrite in spirit,
> and who tremble at my word."

SATURDAY
ROSE WALK
Reading of the Day: Psalm 77:1-12

In 2009, I started taking a "Rose Walk" at the end of my work day. It was my debrief time with God, thanking Him for the sweet flowers in my day and also taking time to entrust to Him the "thorns" - the difficulties I faced. Celeste loved those afternoon walks, because we had no particular path we would follow. We would just go wherever her nose led us, literally walking through the lovely Costa Rican gardens, stopping to smell the roses. I took advantage of those few relaxed moments to reflect on what God was doing for me, in me, around me, and through me.

Take a moment to thank God for the fragrant roses in your day and to recognize the thorns, trusting Him in those areas of life as well.

"I remembered you, God, and I groaned;
I meditated, and my spirit grew faint.
Then I thought, 'To this I will appeal:
I will remember the deeds of the Lord.'"
Selected portions of Psalm 77

SUNDAY
AMAZED ... AT WHAT?
Reading of the Day: Mark 6:1-6

"And He was amazed at their lack of faith."
Mark 6:6a

"I do believe; help me overcome my unbelief!"
Mark 9:24b

Again and again in the gospels, Jesus comments either on people's faith or their lack of it. In Mark 6, Jesus returned to His home town after restoring the demon-possessed man, raising a dead girl, and healing a woman. His "homies," in contrast, questioned His credibility and took offense at Him. In response, Jesus was amazed at their *lack* of faith.

If Jesus were to look at me, I sure hope that He would not be amazed for that reason!

May I amaze You for some other reason today, Lord!

MONDAY
WORD OF THE DAY: EXULT
Reading of the Day: Romans 5:1-8

"And not only this,
but we also exult in our tribulations,
knowing that tribulation brings
about perseverance."
Romans 5:3 NASB

The word *exult* in this passage can also be translated "make boast, glory, joy, rejoice," or even "brag" (*Strong's Greek*).

As Bill McDonald put it, "It is one of the delightful paradoxes of the Christian faith that joy can coexist with affliction… One of the by-products of tribulation is that it produces perseverance or steadfastness. We could never develop perseverance if our lives were trouble-free."

Is your life trouble-free? If not, remember today's key word.

EXULT!

TUESDAY
HEAVENLY *YAPITA*
Reading of the Day: Psalm 94:8-19

"If I should say, 'My foot has slipped,'
Your lovingkindness, O Lord, will hold me up.
When my anxious thoughts multiply within me,
Your consolations delight my soul."
Psalm 94:18-19 NASB

In Bolivia we used to do all our shopping in open markets. Most things were weighed on simple scales—on one side would be placed a half kilo metal weight—or maybe even a rock that weighed about that much. On the other side, the *casera* (vendor) would pile up haba beans or any of the 500+ varieties of potatoes that grow in the Andes Mountains, until the scale was balanced. Then, little Krista or Kari would ask the casera for a *yapita*—just a bit extra thrown in for free. Kari loved to carry her own little market bag where she used to collect all the yapitas to make her own soup once we got home from the market.

Now think of life's scale. Your anxious thoughts weigh down one side. God is willing to heap the other side with His consolations. He not only balances the scale, but adds His heavenly yapita!

WEDNESDAY
YAKETY YAK!
Reading of the Day: Romans 9:14-24

Often I remind you to remember a phrase or verse or song throughout the day. Rarely is it a rock 'n' roll song! But The Coasters came to mind today as I read Romans 9:20:

> "But who are you, O man, to talk back to God?
> Shall what is formed say to him who formed it,
>   'Why did you make me like this?'"

Surely you and I don't talk back to God, do we? We can probably skip over that verse, can't we?

Wait! Think about that a minute! What are ways *you* question God over how He made *you*? Do you wish He'd given you "slim genes"? Made you more extroverted? Given you the gift of teaching? Made you better at Scrabble? How do *you* talk back?

Let these song lyrics help you respond to life in a way that pleases God.

Yakety, Yak... Don't Talk Back!

THURSDAY
WHINER OR GROANER?
Reading of the Day: Romans 8:18-27

"Not only so, but we ourselves,
who have the first fruits of the Spirit,
groan inwardly as we wait eagerly for our adoption
to sonship, the redemption of our bodies."
Romans 8:23

I really try not to be a whiner. When I originally wrote this entry, I was feeling miserable. Remember the word "exult" from a few days ago? Today the focus is on the final word of that verse. Romans 5:3 exhorts us to "exult in our tribulations, knowing that they bring about *perseverance*." If I am a good steward of suffering, I'll grow in perseverance.

All of creation (ourselves included) is groaning along with the Holy Spirit, who "intercedes for us through wordless groans waiting eagerly for our adoption as sons, the redemption of our body." If groaning is good enough for the Holy Spirit, it's good enough for me!

Don't be a whiner! Be a groaner!

FRIDAY
HANGING OUT AT HIS PLACE
Reading of the Day: I Chronicles 16:23-36

"Splendor and majesty are before him;
strength and joy in his dwelling place."
I Chronicles 16:27

What makes one home "cooler" than another? Young people tend to hang out at just a few of their friend's places. Why? Sometimes it's the ambience—like the Krausers' basement all decked out into a 50's style Coke shop. Sometimes it's having "cool parents."

Where would you like to hang out today? Come, hang out at the dwelling place filled with strength and joy. True joy is a by-product of living in His presence. Tell God today, "I want to hang out at *Your* place!"

Breath Prayer of the Day:

Can I hang out at Your place, Lord?

SATURDAY
HE'S ALL YOU NEED
Reading of the Day: II Corinthians 1:7-11

Do you ever feel like life hands you just a bit more than you are capable of managing? You are in good company! Paul says of himself and his traveling ministry companions:

> "We were under great pressure,
> far beyond our ability to endure."
> II Corinthians 1:8

Don't let your mind go down a dead-end alley, comparing your own minuscule trials to the persecutions of Paul! We each have our own limits that God knows very well. And whatever *you* feel like is beyond *your* ability to endure, is your personal limit. And, just like Paul, God will pick you up and carry you through. Just make sure you *trust Him fully* in what you *can't* do, so you can say along with Paul, "But this happened that we might not rely on ourselves but on God, who raises the dead." (v.9)

Father, I know I can lean on You
When I feel like I am wading through life's mire,
Facing its storms and ceaseless waves.
When I come to the end of my rope
With nowhere to turn
Remind me that's exactly the moment I will find that
You are all I need!
I choose today to throw myself absolutely
and wholly on You.

SUNDAY
YES, LORD!
Reading of the Day: II Corinthians 1:12-22

I have a plaque up on my kitchen wall that also graced Grandma Florence's kitchen wall. It simply says, "Yes, Lord."

I have a long history with that simple phrase. For one, it was the key phrase that led us to serve in Costa Rica for sixteen years. Just as my grandmother strove to have her life characterized by obedience to God, so I also want to have that simple phrase represent my life.

Make this phrase into your own breath prayer today:

YES, LORD!

"For the Son of God, Jesus Christ, who was
preached among you by [us]…
was not 'Yes' and 'No,' but in him
it has always been 'Yes.'
For no matter how many promises God has made,
they are 'Yes' in Christ."
II Corinthians 1:19

MONDAY
BREATH PRAYERS
Reading of the Day: Philippians 4:10-19

"Whatever I have, wherever I am,
I can make it through anything in the One who
makes me who I am."
Philippians 4:13 The Message

Yesterday I asked you to pray the breath prayer, "Yes, Lord!" I often write down breath prayers that I can remember throughout my day. Over the next few days, I will suggest a breath prayer for each day. Write it down somewhere to remind you to utter it several times throughout your day. It will bring to life the command, "Pray without ceasing." Amy Carmichael, a missionary to India in the beginning of the 1900's, wrote, "My Lord, my Love, I am content with Thee."

Take a moment right now to think of what implications that prayer has for you today. What issues are you facing? What's on your to-do list? What emotions are you handling? What kind of attitude do you have?

Remind yourself today to pray,

My Lord, my Love, I am content with Thee!

TUESDAY
A LAST NAME THAT PROCLAIMS
Reading of the Day: Acts 4:13-20

When I got married, I thought it would be so much easier to spell R-O-L-A-N-D than S-A-W-T-E-L-L. However, I quickly learned that people can make any name difficult! I'm glad to be Mrs. Woody Roland, but not because of an easy-to-spell last name!

My dad used to tell people to spell our last name, Sawtell, just like the two words, "saw" and "tell," quoting the verse, "That which we have *seen* and heard *declare* we unto you." (I John 1:3)

Acts 4:20 also spells out my maiden name.

"As for us, we cannot help *speaking* [tell] about what we have *seen* [Saw] and heard."

You don't need to remember how to spell my maiden name, but please do remember throughout your day to speak about what you've seen and heard!

WEDNESDAY
DO NOT DISTURB!
Reading of the Day: Genesis 28:10-17

If Christ suddenly showed up during your quiet time, what would you do? If He said, "Don't let me disturb you. I'll just sit here quietly while you continue," would you proceed in the same way?

I've toyed with that thought, and I'm pretty sure that day's quiet time would be radically transformed. Imagine the difference there might be if all doubt of His nearness, love, and attentiveness were removed!

I envy Jacob's experience in Genesis 28:15. In his dream, God vividly told him, "I am with you and will watch over you wherever you go, and I will bring you back to this land. I will not leave you until I have done what I have promised you." Yet, why envy Jacob? We have the Holy Spirit "who is a deposit guaranteeing our inheritance until the redemption of those who are God's possession—to the praise of his glory." Ephesians 1:14

Take time with Him today with a new awareness that *He is present!*

THURSDAY
BIBLICAL SOAP OPERA
Reading of the Day: Genesis 29:31-35

Who needs "As the World Turns," when you can read about the rivalry between Rachel and Leah in Genesis 29 and 30? Both women were desperate for love, security, and happiness. Unfortunately, life does not come with a guarantee of being loved by others, let alone being loved well.

Leah's emotional saga is played out through the naming of her sons. Her firstborn was named Reuben as she expectantly declared, "Surely my husband will love me now!" (Genesis 29:31). By the time Levi came along, she'd given up on the hope of love and was willing to settle for attachment (v. 34). It looked like she finally had the right perspective by the time Judah was born. "This time I will praise the Lord" (v. 35).

Sadly, her whole life was characterized by desperation leading to obsession. How might you be feeling desperate today? Will you sink into obsession or turn and praise the Lord?

FRIDAY
HOLY WHISPERS
Reading of the Day: I Kings 19:9-18

"In the morning, LORD, you hear my voice;
in the morning I lay my requests before you and
wait expectantly."
Psalm 5:3

"After the earthquake came a fire,
but the LORD was not in the fire.
And after the fire came a gentle whisper."
I Kings 19:12

Oftentimes God speaks to us in holy whispers.
Hurry can keep your heart earthbound.

Take an extra moment to quiet your heart before Him
and pray. Give Him time to whisper in your ear!

*May Your thoughts form silently
in the depths of my being
as I wait quietly in Your presence.*

SATURDAY
RUB THE WRONG WAY
Reading of the Day: Romans 15:1-7

St. Therese was a Carmelite religious who became
a nun at age 15 and died of tuberculosis at age 24.

She is known for many of her insights, sayings, poems, prayers, and even plays. She wrote the following account.

"There is one sister in the community who has a knack of rubbing me the wrong way at every turn; her mannerisms, her ways of speaking, her character strike me as unlovable. But then she's a [sister]: God must love her dearly; so I am not going to let my natural dislike of her get the best of me. Thus I remind myself that [Christian] love is not a matter of feelings; it means doing things. I have determined to treat this sister as if she is the person I love best in the world. Every time I meet her, I pray for her and I offer [thanks] to God for her virtues and her efforts. I feel certain that Jesus would like me to do this."

Does this speak to your heart today? Firmly place someone in your mind today. Resolve to treat that individual as if you loved him (or her) best in the world.

PS Just a fun story about St. Therese… She longed to go to heaven by an entirely new way… an elevator that would raise her to Jesus. The elevator would be the arms of Jesus, lifting her "in all her littleness."

SUNDAY
I'D NEVER TAKE REVENGE!
Reading of the Day: Leviticus 19:11-18

"Do not take revenge, my friends…
Overcome evil with good."
Romans 12:19, 21

Most of you are "good Christians," and, if you are like me, you don't really think you need to focus much on God's command not to take revenge. But let's think twice today.

One day I was trying to concentrate in a "quiet zone" of the airport, and two men nearby had been drinking a bit too much. They were loud and boisterous, trying to impress one another as well as everyone else within earshot. As my patience began to grow thin, I approached the men and kindly asked if they could move to another area. Their response was to laugh loudly and ask, "Are *WE* making too much *NOISE*? Are *WE* making too much *NOISE*? Ha, ha, ha!" My reply to this was not exactly ungodly, but it certainly did not fall into the category of "overcoming evil with good!"

I really like what the great scientist, George Washington Carver, had to say: "I will never let another man ruin my life by making me hate him." None of us are exempt from today's Scriptural admonition. Keep this phrase in mind throughout your day today:

OVERCOME EVIL WITH GOOD!

MONDAY
HOW TO TREAT AN ENEMY
Reading of the Day: Matthew 5:44-48

"On the contrary,
'If your enemy is hungry, feed him;
If he is thirsty, give him something to drink,
In doing this, you will heap burning
coals on his head.'"
Romans 12:20

My NIV Bible comments on this passage, saying, "Christian conduct should never betray the high moral standards of the gospel, or it will provoke the disdain of unbelievers and bring the gospel into disrepute."

Pray with me today:

God, please make me aware today of situations in
which I am treated unkindly and unfairly,
And remind me that my response will either bring
You glory or will muddy Your name.
I really want to live like Christ before others today so
that through me and my responses
they might be more open to YOU.

TUESDAY
SOUL TEMP
Reading of the Day: Romans 5:1-11

What is the temperature of your soul today? How's your mood? Are you under a lot of stress? What is going on emotionally in your life? Taking those factors into consideration, is there a yellow, flashing caution light in your life today? If so, it's good to *know* that, in order to be extra aware of the potential of blowing up, over-reacting, saying something inappropriate, having a bad attitude, or just plain not loving people well. Having a fever doesn't excuse wrong behavior.

If you are on edge, take it to God in prayer. Confess your dependence on Him. Ask Him to empower you to be Christ-like today.

"We know that suffering produces perseverance; perseverance, character; and character, hope."
Romans 5:3-4

WEDNESDAY
PERFECT DONOR MATCH
Reading of the Day: Hebrews 4:12-16

"For the word of God is living and active. Sharper than any double-edged sword,

> it penetrates even to dividing soul and spirit,
> joints and marrow;
> it judges the thoughts and attitudes of the heart."
> Hebrews 4:12

Genesis focuses on character change. Abram ("exalted father") became Abraham ("father of many nations"). Jacob ("leg-puller") became Israel ("persevere with God").

Who are you becoming? God knows who you are and not only sees who you can become, but is actively involved in the process of "renaming" you. Hebrews 4:12 tells us God's Word is alive and powerful enough to divide soul and spirit, joints and marrow.

Think about the power of God's Word to divide joints and marrow. The Bible offers deep-seated, name-changing power.

One of the most dramatic cures for cancer is a bone marrow transplant. God's Word is the perfect bone marrow transplant for your character cancers. His Word is able to heal character sickness, making you into a healthy, whole person from the inside out. Christ is the marrow donor, and He is an exact match for you!

THURSDAY
COULD BE WORSE
Reading of the Day: Luke 8:40-56

"It could be worse."
Common Saying in Minnesota

In today's passage from Luke, Jairus, a prominent synagogue leader, came to Jesus pleading, crying, and humiliating himself in front of everyone. His only daughter was dying. His only hope was Jesus. Just at that moment, a woman barged in front of him! Jairus' situation looked bleak, but it was about to turn "bleaker." A messenger arrived, whispering, "Don't bother the Master any longer. It's too late. She's dead."

BUT, the Master overheard! Jesus turned to him and said, "Don't be afraid; just believe."

When your situation goes from bad to worse He says to you,

"I have not forgotten you. Step aside.
I am big enough to handle this.
Despair, disease, and even death are all
under My control.
Don't fear. Only believe."

FRIDAY
SHAKY LEGS
Reading of the Day: Isaiah 54:5-10

"'Though the mountains be shaken
and the hills be removed,
yet my unfailing love for you will not be shaken
nor my covenant of peace be removed,'
says the Lord, who has compassion on you."
Isaiah 54:10

For three years of my life, I rarely had a day when my legs and arms felt steady or when my back did not ache. Rarely had I greeted the dawn thinking, "I feel good today! I'm ready to face any challenge that might come before me!" Instead, morning after morning, I was painfully aware of how desperately weak and needy I was. I admire what Joni Eareckson Tada wrote about her pain and weakness. "The best way to wake up is realizing my desperate need of God's strength."

Whatever your aches and pains, whether they be physical or emotional, God steadies and strengthens you on the path, reminding you, "I chose you. I keep you. And, above all else, I love you." No matter what happens or doesn't happen, you are His beloved.

Make this prayer your own today:

*I am so thankful I am loved by You and
am the apple of Your eye.* (Psalm 17:8)

SATURDAY
NOT FORGOTTEN
Reading of the Day: Isaiah 49:13-16

"But Zion said, 'The LORD has forsaken me, the
Lord has forgotten me.'
Can a mother forget the baby at her breast
and have no compassion on the child she has borne?
Though she may forget, I will not forget you!"
Isaiah 49:14-15

Do you ever feel forgotten, either by people or by
God Himself? Take comfort in the fact that God
knows just how you feel! Over and over in His
Word He talks about being forgotten by His people. No matter if others forget you, you can be assured God will not.

Rest assured today that you are engraved on the
palms of God's hands.

SUNDAY
HEAVENLY FEDEX
Reading of the Day: Psalm 38:15-22

Joni Eareckson Tada is a fan of the "Quickly Psalms." When you need rescuing, deliverance, or an extra dose of "quick grace," dial God's 911.

- "Come quickly to help me, my Lord and my Savior." Psalm 38:22

- "May your mercy come quickly to meet us, for we are in desperate need." Psalm 79:8

- "You are my strength; come quickly to help me." Psalm 22:9

- "Turn your ear to me, come quickly to my rescue; be my rock of refuge, a strong fortress to save me." Psalm 31:2

- "You are my help and my deliverer; LORD, do not delay." Psalm 70:5

Plant firmly in your mind right now to use heavenly FedEx when you need help quickly!

MONDAY
"NO IN THE GARDEN!"
Reading of the Day: Matthew 5:1-12

When Woody and I had the privilege of visiting the Holy Land, I was especially excited about going to a hillside thought to be the location where Jesus spoke to the crowds, teaching them what we now know as The Sermon on the Mount. I had been brushing up on my memorization of Matthew 5-7 with the hope of sitting in the garden, looking down on the Sea of Galilee, and quietly, prayerfully repeating from memory the words of Christ.

Sadly, the moment was spoiled by a person we now look back on as the "Nazi Nun." She stormed through the garden, shooing our group out, shouting at us in her limited English, "No in the garden! No in the garden!" Now whenever I review the opening of Matthew chapter 5, I often laugh, quoting my own paraphrase:

And when He saw the multitude, He went up on the mountain. And, opening His mouth, He began to teach them, saying, "NO IN THE GARDEN!!"

Thankfully, that is not what Jesus did. He sat down, the people gathered around Him, and He taught them. What a privilege it would have been to sit at His feet and hear those words!

TUESDAY
TO DO AND NOT TO DO,
THAT IS THE QUESTION
Reading of the Day: Luke 6:37-38; 13:32-35

"Do not judge, and you will not be judged."
Luke 6:37

Come sit with me in the garden (ignoring the Nazi Nun), and meditate on what we are NOT to do and what we ARE to do.

Luke 6:37 tells us to just say, "**NO!**" There should be NO focusing on the failures and weaknesses of others. It is so easy to take very seriously what others do wrong and to be quick to judge them. As you see people around you today, evaluate your response to them and choose the YES! option, rather than the "judging option" that comes so naturally to each one of us.

Jesus was overwhelmed with emotion on various occasions. To me, the occasion described in Luke 13 is one of the most touching examples. Jesus modeled for us the concept of **YES!** Before His death, Jesus looked down on Jerusalem and cried, "How often I have longed to gather your children together, as a hen gathers her chicks under her wings, and you were not willing." Luke 13:34

Keep your eyes open to the needs of the world around you. Be sensitive today to say **NO** to judging others, and **YES** to an overwhelming sense of compassion for them. Jesus gives us a whole new perspective on a lost world!

WEDNESDAY
YES AND NO
Reading of the Day: Romans 12:9-21

Meditate on another set of Biblical mandates for what you should and shouldn't do today.

NO!

Do not be self-righteous or critical. Put aside your fault-finding spirit. *Don't* look at others' faults with a microscope and your own with a telescope. *Don't* look down on others. Remember the Pharisee and tax collector, and *don't* pray, "God, I thank you that I am not like other men!" (Luke 18:10-14).

YES!

Ask God for a compassionate, forgiving spirit. "Forgive as the Lord forgave you." (Colossians 3:13) Esteem others better than yourself.

"In humility consider others better than yourselves."
Philippians 2:3

THURSDAY
MY INDEPENDENCE!
Reading of the Day: Galatians 6:1-10

"Carry each other's burdens."
Galatians 6:2

Parents of young children often have to say, "**NO!**" Part of parenting is also saying and modeling the positive things. Here are a couple of things our Heavenly Father says to us.

NO!

Do not have an independent, self-sufficient spirit. In the USA we treasure our independence. That can be a good thing, but sometimes it can become an obstacle in our walk with Christ.

"If I must boast, I will boast of the things that show my weakness." II Corinthians 11:30

YES!

Depend upon Him and recognize your need for others.

"Trust God from the bottom of your heart;
don't try to figure out everything on your own.
Listen for God's voice in everything you do,
everywhere you go;

he's the one who will keep you on track.
Don't assume that you know it all."
Proverbs 3:6

FRIDAY
ANOTHER DAY OF YES AND NO
Reading of the Day: I Samuel 13:7-14

NO!

We must say 'no' to the temptation to follow our own ways or insist on our own timing. Try instead to listen and follow *God's* timing and *God's* leading. Personally, I find that it's difficult (if not impossible), to understand the timing of the One who does not rule by the calendar or clock. King Saul was very impatient when Samuel did not show up for the sacrifice. So, he took things into his own hands. That turned out to be the final blow for poor King Saul.

YES!

David was far from perfect as king, yet he was "a man after God's own heart." We can catch a glimpse of the hearts of these two men when we observe the final years of Saul's life. He dedicated his energy to destroying David. In a dramatic contrast, upon hearing of Saul's death, David sincerely mourns the nation's loss, though this was the very man who had been trying to take his life. David cried out, "Your glory, O Israel, lies slain on your heights. How the mighty have fallen!" II Samuel 1:19.

Lord. I may not understand Your timing or Your ways,
but I choose to trust you and say,
"Yes, Lord!"

SATURDAY
NO, NO, NO!
Reading of the Day: II Corinthians 12:7-10

When I faced several years of pain and disability, I had many people praise me for being so strong. Rarely did I compare myself to the Apostle Paul, but I think he would agree with my inner response to those well-intended, kind words noting my strength in the face of adversity. "No, no, no! You don't get it! I am not strong at all! He is strong! And the only way you see me as strong is that in my greatest weakness, He shows Himself strong." My strength comes from my weakness, and that's no false modesty!

Few can imagine the many times I have cried out in my great weakness. My most common prayer during those years was, "Help me! Help me! Help me!" The Scottish preacher, James Stewart (not to be confused with the actor Jimmy Stewart!), put it this way: "It is always upon human weakness and humiliation, not human strength and confidence, that God chooses to build His Kingdom; and that He can use us not merely in spite of our ordinariness and helplessness and disqualifying infirmities, but precisely because of them."

Take a moment to think of what you might name as your "disqualifying infirmities." Then take time to thank God for the opportunity to see Him show Himself strong in your weakness.

Once you are convinced of your own weakness
and no longer trying to hide it,
you embrace the power of Christ.
—Charles Swindoll

SUNDAY
IS THAT ALL?
Reading of the Day: I Corinthians 4:8-16

"I am not writing this to shame you…"
I Corinthians 4:14

Paul wrote that he didn't mean to make them feel bad when he listed the following in a matter of just five verses.

I have been made a spectacle before both men and angels. I am a fool for Christ. I am held in disrepute, considered weak, hungry, thirsty, poor, homeless, over-worked, cursed, persecuted and slandered. I have become like garbage, the scum of the earth.

Is that all?!?

Paul was not boasting of his sufferings or calling on the Corinthians to join a pity party. Instead, he was calling on them as his spiritual children to join him in protecting the reputation of the gospel. He not only warned them as a diligent father to avoid false teaching, but also called on them to join him in his imitation of Christ.

If you face a long list of difficulties today, don't send out RSVP's for a pity party. Let them motivate you to imitate Christ.

MONDAY
THANKS, BUT NO THANKS!
Reading of the Day: Isaiah 41:10-13

"I rise before dawn and cry for help;
I hope in Your words."
Psalm 119:147

Would you even think, let alone dare, to say to God, "I can manage today on my own. No need for You today, thank You."? Yet how often are we saying just that without actually uttering those words? The enemy subtly deceives us into trying to live out our lives independent of God. Satan doesn't even mind if we fill our schedules with spiritual activities, as long as we run on our own steam instead of living in conscious dependence on the Spirit's power.

King David knew, despite his power, that he was nothing without God. Again and again he cries out, turning his heart to God in prayer. "In the morning you hear my voice." Psalm 5:3 "In the morning my prayer comes before you." Psalm 88:13 "My soul waits for the Lord more than the watchmen for the morning." Psalm 130:6

If King David couldn't do it on his own, who do we think *we* are to take the day on without reliance upon God?

TUESDAY
THE FIERCELY JEALOUS LOVER
Reading of the Day: James 4:4-10

"The proverb has it that
'He is a fiercely jealous lover.'" The Message
"God opposes the proud but
shows favor to the humble." NIV
(Two versions of James 4:6)

Yesterday's entry addressed our tendency to try to manage our lives on our own. According to God's book, our bent toward self-sufficiency simply boils down to pride. God detests pride. Pride has been aptly called "the complete anti-God state of mind." It is like a cancer that slowly consumes the soul.

Since there is no sin more offensive to Him, we had better be on guard to avoid it.

In contrast, God pours out His grace on the humble. Instead of relying on our self-sufficiency, if we humbly kneel at the foot of the cross and look up, we will catch a glimpse of the magnitude of His loving sacrifice. Fixing our eyes on the undeserved gift of salvation, we come to realize the greatness of God and the smallness of man. Humble your heart before God, thanking Him for the depth of His love for you.

> "I, the Lord your God, am a jealous God…
> Showing love to a thousand generations of those
> who love me and keep my commandments."
> Exodus 20:5-6

WEDNESDAY
BOARD OR LORD?
Reading of the Day: James 1:1-8

"I serve at the pleasure of the board." This statement reflects the fact that the person is not his own boss. He is not only accountable to a higher authority, but also is there to carry out the wishes and priorities of the one who hired him.

Time and again we see this concept reflected as the writers of the New Testament books identify themselves. In Romans 1:1 Paul calls himself "a servant of Christ." Peter writes that he is "a servant and apostle of Jesus Christ." (II Peter 1:1) Jude also says he is "a servant of Jesus Christ." (Jude 1:1) Even Jesus' half-brother James made no claim to fame as family, but chose instead to identify himself as a servant of God and of the Lord Jesus. (James 1:1)

Each of them considered it an honor and privilege to be counted as a bond servant of Christ. They might have even phrased it, "I serve at the pleasure of the Lord."

It is indeed a pleasure to serve at the pleasure of the Lord!

THURSDAY
DON'T THANK YOUR LUCKY STARS!
Reading of the Day: John 3:25-30

"A person cannot receive even one thing unless it
is given him from heaven."
John 3:27

It is good to have an attitude of gratitude. But have you ever thought about the object of your thankfulness? Think about the saying, "I thank my lucky stars!" I'd like to challenge you to thank the *creator* of the stars.

Being thankful without an object of our gratitude is like throwing things up to the empty sky. It is certainly good to express our gratitude to the *people* around us. But as we can see from today's Bible reading, every good thing comes from our gracious and loving *Father*.

Think of something you are thankful for right now and imagine it in your clasped hand. Now imagine tossing that up into the air. Keep that image in your mind today as you refuse to toss it to your lucky stars, but instead direct your thankfulness to your Heavenly Father.

FRIDAY
FEAR OF GOD, FEAR OF ALLAH
Reading of the Day: Psalm 130:1-4

"But there is forgiveness with You,
That You may be feared."
Psalm 130:4

The idea that God is love is inconceivable to a Muslim. Allah is seen as a god who is angry with man. He demands sacrifices of prayer five times a day, giving alms, making a pilgrimage to Mecca, fasting during Ramadan, and jihad—all done in an attempt to appease him. Everything is "if Allah wills," living without hope; their lives controlled by fear.

By contrast, Jesus, out of pure love, voluntarily gave His life in order to offer us forgiveness and an abundant life. For a Muslim, nobody gives his life for another. But for us, privileged children of God, His sacrifice on our behalf and His unfathomable forgiveness leads us to fall on our knees in awe and joyful worship.

Aren't you glad you are a God-fearer rather than a fearful follower of Allah?

SATURDAY
CONFIDENCE IN MOTION
Reading of the Day: Acts 17:24-29

"In Him we live and move and have our being."
Acts 17:28

We have been watching the construction of a new Subaru dealership in our neighborhood. It's a multi-faceted project, and the building and landscaping are impressive. Watching each new phase of this project has started me thinking about Subaru's slogan, "Confidence in Motion." This motto provides a great parallel to our spiritual lives.

Trust is not really trust without taking action. If I say, "I trust you can carry me," but I refuse to let you pick me up, is that really trust?

I don't know how much confidence I can put in a Subaru, but I know whose hands are worthy of my trust. Put your hand in His today and walk with Him. Post a note today to remind yourself of the phrase, "confidence in motion."

SUNDAY
A TWIST ON TRUST
Reading of the Day: Genesis 6:11-14, 22

While going through years of trial, I often read or heard, "Someday you will look back and see how much closer to God you have grown through this." Or, a corollary is, "You develop more Christ-like character through times like these." I agree that sometimes God grows us through trusting Him in the hard times. But there is a deeper trust level when we choose to walk by faith even if we never know and never understand.

Noah was a man of faith because he trusted God's word and built the ark in spite of the ridicule of others. He was proved right when the floodwaters rose. But what if he died without ever seeing the rain, yet still chose to trust and obey?

We don't all live to see the rain. However, if we make the simple choice to obey, irrespective of the outcome, we bring honor to God.

MONDAY
THE LAST WORD
Reading of the Day: I Corinthians 15:53-58

"Who got the last word, oh, Death?
Oh, Death, who's afraid of you now?"
I Corinthians 15:5 The Message

How can I write a devotional entry as I sit beside my dad at midnight, watching him take his final breaths? Yet, what better spot is there to marvel at the defeat of death, the wonder of hope, and the power of the resurrection?

The introduction to this book included a quote from my dad, "We become like what we worship."

Dad, it's a privilege to watch you as you take the final step on earth to become like the One you and I worship. So, even on this sad day in my life, I rejoice that this isn't the end. Thanks to our Savior, it's a glorious beginning.

TUESDAY
HIS GRACE IS ENOUGH
Reading of the Day: II Corinthians 12:6-10

In the midst of "Balrog," I went through some dreadful days while going through the pain clinic for several weeks. One of the principles that had to be followed during those weeks was to make a schedule of activities and stick to it. So, despite my desire to stay in bed and wallow in self-pity, I went to church with my friend Helen. We sat in the far back in case I just couldn't make it through the service. The first worship song was "His Grace is Enough." I could not sing those words. Turning to Helen in tears, I whispered, "It just doesn't seem to be enough for me today."

As the service continued, I read lyrics to songs and portions of Scripture on the screen in front and sensed God nudging me, saying, "What you see is truth, whether you feel it or not."

I joined in, singing and reading the Scripture aloud with the congregation with a new conviction to speak out what I know is true.

Remind yourself to thank God throughout your day that:

His grace is enough!

WEDNESDAY
Teşekkür Ederim
Reading of the Day: Ephesians 5:15-20

Don't feel like thanking God today? ***Good!***

"He who sacrifices thank offerings honors me."
Psalm 50:23

Sacrifice: The act of losing or surrendering
something.

In our day-to-day lives, we rarely think we are making a sacrifice when we simply say, "thank you." When we were in Turkey for 11 days in 2010, I was determined to learn to say "thank you" in Turkish. It was not easy: "Teşekkür Ederim." Let me tell you, it was a sacrifice for me to give thanks in Turkish!

Some days it is hard to be thankful to God. But those are the days we can offer up a precious, pleasing sacrifice. Take a moment to thank Him for at least ten things right now!

"Sing songs from your heart to Christ. Sing praises
over everything,
any excuse for a song to God the Father in the
name of our Master, Jesus Christ."
Ephesians 5:19 The Message

THURSDAY
HEAVENLY WHIFFLE BALL BAT
Reading of the Day: Romans 8:26-30

One year we hosted a birthday party with one piñata for the adults and one for the children. It was really a fun celebration. One thing happened that day that has served me in my prayer life. After many had taken their turn with the whiffle ball bat, whacking the piñata, it finally cracked and showered down candies. As usual, everyone scrambled to pick up as many as they could, but the boy with the bat in hand made a huge sweep with the bat, gathering almost every single candy for himself in one wide swoop.

Sometimes when I don't know how to pray, I picture all the friends and family I want to pray for and tell God, "I sweep them all up with my bat to give them all to You."

Give it a try today. Close your eyes, picture all those you want to pray for, and use your heavenly whiffle ball bat.

FRIDAY
A SELFIE LIFE
Reading of the Day: Colossians 3:12-17

On June 22, 2015, I was watching the Semi-Finals of the Copa America Centenario in Chicago. In that important game, Chile's soccer team beat Colombia. There was an incredible storm during half-time, so there was a game delay over two hours long. As the teams and fans sought shelter, the cable network showed replays of the US-Argentina game. (The US was routed 0-4 in that game, in case you want to know.) When the storm abated, and as they tried to clear standing water from the field, the cameras started panning the waiting crowd and zooming in on fans from both countries.

One element of our current society was blatantly evident. Most of the fans were self-absorbed, phones in hand to take selfies. Unaware of the cameras filming them, they would primp themselves and smile into their phones. At an event where a country unites behind its soccer team, you would think there would be a great sense of community. Instead, what I observed was a stadium full of around 67,000 self-absorbed individuals.

Think about it today... are you living a "selfie life" or one that flips the camera to zoom in on others?

SATURDAY
A JEALOUS MISSIONARY
Reading of the Day: Matthew 4:22-25

Our kids grew up listening to the radio program called "Odyssey." I, too, loved to listen and imagine myself magically transported back in Biblical times to observe firsthand significant events in history.

Matthew 4:23 says, "And some were in great pain... Jesus healed them all." If you were in that crowd, what would you have asked Jesus to heal? A sore throat? Depression? A chronic illness? Surely there would have been *something* each and every person present would want healed.

Though "He healed them all," there were people in other communities that were *not* healed. There were people *before* Jesus' ministry began that never experienced healing, and there were others, like us, who came along much later. Even for those who were healed that day, they went on to face failing health and eventual death.

I do not have the answers to the dilemma of pain. But I know we are called to go to Jesus and trust. He can heal you. And if He doesn't, He is still worthy of your trust and praise. Make this your prayer today.

Lord, I trust You to either heal me or give me grace to bear my infirmities.

SUNDAY
JUGGLING LIFE
Reading of the Day: Colossians 3:15-25

Do you ever find it hard to juggle all the things going on in your life?

I do. But I've found two words that make life more do-able when it gets complicated. *Now* and *next*.

Those are the only two things I need to keep in mind. Do well what is in front of me now. And keep in mind what I will do well next. Then the other things will fall into place.

"Whatever you do, work at it with all your heart, as working for the Lord, not for men, since you know that you will receive an inheritance from the Lord as a reward.
It is the Lord Christ you are serving."
Colossians 3:23-24

Whatever you are doing *now*, do it with all your heart! Then, when *that* is done, whatever is *next*, do *it* with your whole heart!

MONDAY
PRAYER AT THE POINT OF ANXIETY
Reading of the Day: Psalm 34:1-8

"Don't fret or worry. Instead of worrying, pray. Let petitions and praises shape your worries into prayers, letting God know your concerns. Before you know it, a sense of God's wholeness, everything coming together for good, will come and settle you down.
It's wonderful what happens when Christ displaces worry at the center of your life."
Philippians 4:6-7 The Message

If you want to control your life, try anxiety. It won't work, but you can try! A better alternative is to seek God in prayer at every point of your anxiety. God promises that works!

Prayer turns off the valve that pumps
anxiety into our souls.
Persist until peace comes.

"God met me more than half way,
he freed me from my anxious fears."
Psalm 34:4 The Message

TUESDAY
EVEN IF
Reading of the Day: Psalm 25: 1-10

"To you, O Lord, I lift up my soul.
O my God, in you I trust." Psalm 25:1-2

There have been times I have identified with the psalmist in saying, "On you I wait all the day long." And when I say that, I mean, "Where in the world *are* You, O God?" Life sometimes hits us with blow after blow, absolutely exhausting us. At times like that, let's learn to pause and consider, "What am I hoping in?" Many times our hopes are pinned on a certain outcome.

I love the example of Shadrach, Meshach, and Abednego in Daniel 3. They boldly declare to the king the power of their God. And then they add, "Even if He does not rescue us, we want you as king to know that we will not serve your gods or worship the gold statue you set up." (Daniel 3:17-18)

Their hope was not pinned on a certain outcome. Their hope was in God Himself. Their outcome might change, but God would not. He was worthy of their complete trust.

Consider today where your hopes are pinned. Take a moment to pray—not asking for a specific outcome, but declaring your trust in God.

WEDNESDAY
HOPE VS HOPELESSNESS
Reading of the Day: Luke 23:39-43

The first time I met Norma was in La Paz, Bolivia, at the time of the death of her father. Her mother had died several years earlier. Later, Norma became our adopted daughter.

In La Paz, the burials are done above ground in crypts that generally stack five rows high. This form of above ground burial takes advantage of limited space to provide for a large population with limited space.

On that day, we were not the only small group in the cemetery bidding farewell to a loved one. But, there was a huge contrast between our cluster of believers and the other mourners who did not have the assurance of heaven. Norma's older sister, who had recently put her trust in Christ, gave a heartfelt message of hope through faith in Jesus. The other groups nearly drowned Toty out with their wailing and shouting. Their hopelessness painted a clear contrast to the hope found in Jesus Christ.

As Jesus turned to the criminal next to Him on the cross, He gave him hope in his final hour of torment, saying, "Today you will be with me in paradise."

Let's not take for granted the hope that is ours because of what Jesus has done for you and me!

Appendix A:
Lent

Remember, Lent begins every year on Ash Wednesday and ends the Saturday right before Resurrection Sunday. It's easy to find the dates. Google "Dates Lent 2019" or whatever year you are in. I'd suggest you make note somewhere of when to pause in the regular calendar to switch to the entries for Lent.

You may not be familiar with the Lent tradition. If you are, this type of fast/feast is probably totally different from those you've known in the past. The purpose of Lent is to prepare your heart through prayer, meditation, and self-denial. Rather than encouraging you to give up chocolate or some other treasured element of your day, this portion of the calendar prompts you to give up those things we treasure in our hearts which are not pleasing to God and replace them with qualities that honor Him.

May the next 40 days be life-transforming for you. Get ready to fast!

FYI: The Sunday entries are dedicated to celebrating our new life in Christ, rather than fasting. Traditionally only feasting, not fasting, has been observed on Sundays during Lent.

ASH WEDNESDAY
LENT: DAY 1
Reading of the Day: Matthew 7:1-5

Let's start out our spiritual fast
today with these principles:

FAST FROM JUDGING OTHERS
FEAST ON CHRIST DWELLING IN THEM

"Do not judge, or you too will be judged.
For in the same way you judge others,
you will be judged,
and with the measure you use,
it will be measured to you."
Matthew 7:1-2

I once had a very difficult boss. She used guilt-mongering as her primary management style. One day I had an epiphany. She was so difficult because she was very needy and insecure. Once I reframed her behavior in my mind, I found I was able to see her and respond to her as an individual in need of Christ.

Try to reframe your understanding of others today. Every face has a trace of God's artistry!

THURSDAY
LENT: DAY 2
Reading of the Day: Luke 9:49-56

FAST FROM REACTING
FEAST ON CHRIST-LIKE RESPONDING

"Desire without knowledge is not good—
how much more will hasty feet miss the way!"
Proverbs 19:2

I always say that thinking on my feet is not my forte. My only wise responses come after a pause for reflection. But I am sure "good" at reacting!

I once read a book called *Three Seconds—The Power of Thinking Twice.* The back cover says, "Just three seconds. The time it takes to make a decision."

Take a moment to reflect on today's passage from Luke 9, observing the disciples' *reactions* and Jesus' *responses.* When you read the gospels, pray that you may do so with a teachable heart, learning from how Jesus *responded* to people and situations.

My challenge to you (and ME!) in today's fast/feast is to allow at least three seconds to respond—*not* react. Pray that your responses would reflect Christ.

FRIDAY
LENT: DAY 3
Reading of the Day: Ephesians 5:1-7

FAST FROM WORDS THAT POLLUTE
FEAST ON SPEECH THAT EDIFIES

"Watch the way you talk. Let nothing foul or dirty
come out of your mouth.
Say only what helps, each word a gift."
Ephesians 4:29 The Message

The world around us is focused on climate change
and pollution. I agree that we have failed in our
God-granted responsibility to be good stewards of
the earth. But what would this world be like if we
paid half as much attention to **words** that pollute?

Focus today on climate change—create a verbal climate that edifies!

SATURDAY
LENT: DAY 4
Reading of the Day: Philippians 2:1-4
(See below)

FAST FROM PROTECTING YOUR RIGHTS
AND REPUTATION
FEAST ON SELF-DENIAL

> "If you've gotten anything at all
> out of following Christ,
> if his love has made any difference in your life,
> if being in a community of the
> Spirit means anything to you,
> if you have a heart, if you care—
> then do me a favor:
> Agree with each other, love each other,
> be deep-spirited friends.
> Don't push your way to the front;
> don't sweet-talk your way to the top.
> Put yourself aside, and help others get ahead.
> Don't be obsessed with getting
> your own advantage.
> Forget yourselves long enough to
> lend a helping hand."
> Philippians 2:1-4 The Message

Woody and I wrote our own wedding vows. Sadly, I don't think we have a copy or recording of the exact words! However, I do know my vows included surrendering my rights to Woody.

Easier said than done!

What rights are you clinging to that God wants you to surrender?

SUNDAY
FAST FROM FASTING!
Reading of the Day: I Corinthians 15:1-8

FAST FROM FASTING
FEAST ON THE RESURRECTION!

The early Christians saw Christ's resurrection as a new creation, and so they transferred the Sabbath from Saturday to Sunday. Since all Sundays—and not simply Easter Sunday—were days to celebrate Christ's resurrection, Christians were forbidden to fast and do other forms of penance on those days. Therefore, when the Church expanded the period of fasting and prayer in preparation for Easter from a few days to 40 days (to mirror Christ's fasting in the desert), Sundays could not be included in the count.

All that to say that on Sundays, we will be "fasting from fasting." Focus today on the glorious power of the resurrection!

> "I want to know Christ and the
> power of his resurrection."
> Philippians 3:10a

MONDAY
LENT: DAY 5
Reading of the Day: II Timothy 1:3-12

FAST FROM TIMIDITY
FEAST ON POWER, LOVE, AND
SELF-DISCIPLINE

"For God did not give us a spirit of timidity,
but a spirit of power, of love and of self-discipline."
II Timothy 1:7

Humor me for a moment as I speak to those of
you who are shy, like me. (Listen in, those who
aren't.) Paul is not exhorting us to become ex-
troverts. Actually, being shy can sometimes allow
us to speak powerfully into other people's lives.
Listen well to people. Prepare your mind for any
opportunity that might present itself today. You
might keep a small note card in hand—jotting
down thoughts based on what God is teaching
you. Pray that God will help you listen to others
today and show you an opportune moment to
humbly and lovingly share His truth with someone else.

TUESDAY
LENT: DAY 6
Reading of the Day: Romans 12:9-21

FAST FROM SELFISHNESS
FEAST ON BEING MINDFUL OF THE NEEDS
OF OTHERS

"Be devoted to one another in brotherly love.
Honor one another above yourselves."
Romans 12:10

Woody's family has a memorized prayer which I have grown to love over the years. It includes the phrase, "Help us to be ever mindful of the needs of others." As our children were growing up, I would often ask them, "How can you be mindful of the needs of others today?" That's my question for you today!

Lord, help me to look self-stuff straight
in the face and nail it to the cross.
Remind me today to be ever mindful
of the needs of others!

WEDNESDAY
LENT: DAY 7
Reading of the Day: James 1:19-25

FAST FROM ANGER
FEAST ON PATIENCE

Kiddingly, I often share my own convenient paraphrase of James 1:19-20: "Be quick to speak, quick to anger, and slow to listen." Now if that were the Bible's exhortation, I'd be doing well. However, that's not what we are called to do. I like this version from The Message:

"Lead with your ears, follow up with your tongue,
    and let anger straggle along in the rear.
God's righteousness doesn't grow from human anger."

As you practice your fast and feast today, remember to lead with your ears!

THURSDAY
LENT: DAY 8
Reading of the Day: Philippians 2:12-18

FAST FROM WHINGING
FEAST ON EXPRESSING APPRECIATION

"Do everything without complaining or arguing."
Philippians 2:14

No, I did not misspell "whinging!" I love how the British say "whinging" (pronounced with a short i and rhymes with "cringing.") It's always hard to teach children not to whinge. But adults make good whingers, too!

Woody is a great example to me of expressing appreciation. If anyone can come up with a positive side of a person, it is my dear husband. Jesus, of course, is our best example. Life *really* wasn't fair for him. Yet he did not utter a word about injustice toward Himself.

Think of the times you would have complained if you had been in Jesus' sandals. How did He model a life without whinging?

FRIDAY
LENT: DAY 9
Reading of the Day: II Corinthians 10:1-5

FAST FROM NEGATIVE SELF-TALK
FEAST ON THE VOICE OF THE HOLY SPIRIT

"We demolish arguments and every pretension
that sets itself up against the knowledge of God,
and we take captive every thought to make it
obedient to Christ."
II Corinthians 10:5

Taking thoughts captive requires exercising our faith muscles. Most of us exercise our bodies regularly—or *wish* we did so! But how often do you think of exercising your faith muscles? Perhaps you struggle with thoughts that take *you* captive rather than you actually taking *them* captive. Exercise your faith muscles today, and keep exercising regularly!

SATURDAY
LENT: DAY 10
Reading of the Day: I Peter 5:5-11

FAST FROM PRIDE
FEAST ON HUMILITY

"God has had it with the proud,
But takes delight in just plain people."
I Peter 5:5 The Message

Don't make the same mistake I once made. I got to thinking, "Pride isn't the issue I struggle with." That very day I was humbled—big time! We all struggle with pride, whether we recognize it or not!

Make it your goal in life to reflect the character and priorities of Christ. A good place to start on that today is to have a humble heart. Paul appealed to the Corinthians by the "meekness and gentleness of Christ." (II Cor. 10:1) Let that characterize your life today.

SUNDAY
TRUST THE HAND
Reading of the Day: 1 Peter 2:21-25

In the midst of grave suffering, Jesus surrendered completely to His Father. In today's passage, Peter uses the example of Jesus to show us how we should follow in His footsteps when facing our own trials. Suffering is a given in this life, but in the midst of our greatest trials, we are given the option to entrust ourselves—our will, our desires, our life—to the loving hands of our mighty God, believing He will redeem that suffering for His ultimate glory. We may not see an obvious "good outcome" when making that choice.

The outcome Jesus saw that day was mockery, beatings, and an eventual cruel death. In His final hours, Jesus did not turn to His Father to ask Him to stop the suffering. He chose to trust the hand of the One who allowed it in the first place. As a result, all of mankind now has access to redemption.

If you are facing a trial today, turn to the One who deserves your trust. Like David, you will be able to say,

"I would have lost heart, unless
I believed that I would see
the goodness of the Lord in the land of the living."
(Psalm 27:13)

MONDAY
LENT: DAY 11
Reading of the Day: Colossians 3:1-4

FAST FROM NEGATIVES
FEAST ON ALTERNATIVES

"So if you're serious about living this new
resurrection life with Christ, act like it.
Pursue the things over which Christ presides.
Don't shuffle along, eyes to the ground, absorbed
with the things right in front of you.
Look up, and be alert to what is going on around
Christ—that's where the action is.
See things from his perspective."
Colossians 3:1 The Message.

Focusing on the reality of our citizenship in heaven
allows us to take our focus off the negatives, and
see things from a different perspective. Take time to
think through a difficult situation or relationship
you are facing, and ask God to give you an alternative point of view today.

TUESDAY
LENT: DAY 12
Reading of the Day: Ephesians 4:25-32

FAST FROM BITTERNESS
FEAST ON FORGIVENESS

"Get rid of all bitterness...Be kind and
compassionate to one another,
forgiving each other, just as in
Christ God forgave you."
Ephesians 4:31-32

Do you have any deep, hidden bitter spots in your heart? Every once in a while, I get a glimpse into a spot or two in my own heart. If I take a moment to think about it, it's scary to realize that I can hide a spot that will find an opportunity to rear its ugly head, welling up into emotions, attitudes, and behaviors that can be powerfully dangerous.

Ask God to reveal to you any bitter spots and replace them with His healing forgiveness. Offer that forgiveness to whoever you might be blaming for your own bitterness.

WEDNESDAY
LENT: DAY 13
Reading of the Day: Hebrews 12:7-13

FAST FROM WEAK KNEES
FEAST ON STRAIGHT PATHS

"Therefore, strengthen your feeble
arms and weak knees.
Make level paths for your feet,
so that the lame may not be disabled,
but rather healed."
Hebrews 12:12-13

Sometimes we need a coach to tell us, "Be strong! You can do it!" I feel like that's the message in the verses above. You may feel like you can't go on, but strengthen those feeble arms and weak knees! Catch your second wind. Head in the right direction, and GO in His power!

THURSDAY
LENT: DAY 14
Reading of the Day: Colossians 3:5-14

FAST FROM SELF-CONCERN
FEAST ON COMPASSION

The old self includes a lot of negative things like anger, rage, malice, slander, filthy language, impurity, lust, evil desires, and greed. If you were to categorize it with one small four-letter word, that word would be:

SELF

The Bible speaks a lot about putting off the old self. My mentor, Win, once told me that one of the big goals in her marriage was to eliminate selfishness. Now that's a big goal!

As you shed that four-letter word, **SELF,** today, remember the clothes you are encouraged to put on...

"Clothe yourselves with compassion."
Colossians 3:12

FRIDAY
LENT: DAY 15
Reading of the Day: Matthew 18:15-20

FAST FROM SUSPICION
FEAST ON TRUTH

You can break the habit of destructive thought patterns that damage relationships. Ask yourself, "What is true?"

Matthew 18:15 says, "If a fellow believer hurts you, go and tell him—work it out between the two of you. If he listens, you've made a friend." The Message

If you have a problem with someone, you are responsible to talk to that person about it. In your times with God, He can help you realize how you might have hurt or offended someone, even if that person has *not* come to *you,* and you need to go to *him*. Spend your energy learning truth from God's Word about what your attitudes and actions should be towards others.

SATURDAY
LENT: DAY 16
Reading of the Day: Proverbs 11:11-13

FAST FROM GOSSIP
FEAST ON PURPOSEFUL SILENCE

"A gossip betrays a confidence;
so avoid anyone who talks too much."
Proverbs 20:19

In the church there are some sins we find easier to condemn than others. I'm sure you can think of examples in today's Christian culture. But when did you last hear someone protest against gossip? Yet gossip has probably divided and destroyed more churches than any other sin!

Gossip is one sin that requires two people... one to talk and one to listen. Fast from gossip today... not just the talking part, but partnering in it as well.

SUNDAY
REMEDY FOR DISCOURAGEMENT
Reading of the Day: Psalm 95:1-7

Discouragement is an effective tool of the enemy. Oftentimes, it seems impossible to avoid discouragement. But intentional praise is a powerful defense. Several years ago, Win challenged me to start my day with praise. Based on that advice, I try to begin my day by listing at least ten things I am thankful for. Take a moment right now to express to God your thankfulness for at least ten things.

"Come, let's shout praises to God,
raise the roof for the Rock who saved us!

Let's march into his presence singing praises."
Psalm 95:2 The Message

Becky Harling, the author of *The 30 Day Praise Challenge*, says, "Praising God is not a glib response when life's circumstances are going well. Praising God is an intentional act of faith that affirms our trust in God, even when life is not going well. As we praise Him, our souls are transformed."

MONDAY
LENT: DAY 17
Reading of the Day: Philippians 4:4-9

FAST FROM PROBLEMS THAT OVERWHELM
FEAST ON PRAYER THAT SUSTAINS

"Be anxious for nothing, but in everything by
prayer and supplication with thanksgiving,
let your requests be made known to God."
Philippians 4:6 NASB

Problems tend to bowl us over like huge waves. We come spluttering up, with seaweed hanging from our hair and salt water pouring out our nose and ears. Everything tastes of salt and sand.

When I nearly drowned several years ago on Playa Cahuita in Costa Rica, Woody's words turned my focus from the very real presence of unending, powerful waves to purposeful effort that propelled me to shore.

Forget the waves. Swim in prayer!

TUESDAY
LENT: DAY 18
Reading of the Day: Philippians 3:17 – 4:1

FAST FROM PERIPHERALS
FEAST ON JESUS

"Their mind is set on earthly things.
But our citizenship is in heaven.
And we eagerly await a Savior from there,
the Lord Jesus Christ."
Philippians 3:19-20

Our minds and attention are so easily caught up in the "realities" surrounding us.

When the world around us hits us with all five senses, it is challenging to remember God has already seated us in the heavenly realms with Christ. Our life truly is hidden with Christ in God. Just try to wrap your mind around *that* today!! As you go through your day, make this your prayer:

God, is this peripheral? How can I see Jesus in this?

WEDNESDAY
LENT: DAY 19
Reading of the Day: I Samuel 13:7-14

FAST FROM THE URGENT
FEAST ON THE IMPORTANT

"Saul waited seven days, the time set by Samuel,
but Samuel did not come to Gilgal.
And the people were leaving him. So Saul said,
'Bring me the burnt gift and the peace gifts.'"
I Samuel 13:8

Saul's downfall in today's passage was that he was focused on the urgent. Think about his situation a moment. The urgent not only seemed very urgent, but very important. But what he chose wasn't important enough. It cost him his kingship.

Sometimes I feel like a slave to my inbox. Google mail has a feature that you can sort your inbox into what is very important and "the rest." I find, however, that if I mark something "important," it tends to get left a long time. Why? I know that if it's that important, it probably requires time and effort, so maybe I'd better deal with it later. (Maybe that's not such a wise approach?!?)

Remember today to feast on what is important in God's eyes.

THURSDAY
LENT: DAY 20
Reading of the Day: Ephesians 2:11-20

FAST FROM FAMILIARITY
FEAST ON BEING A STRANGER

"You are no longer foreigners and strangers,
but fellow citizens with God's people."
Ephesians 2:19

It is not scientific doubt, not atheism,
not pantheism, not agnosticism,
that in our day and in this land is likely
to quench the light of the gospel.
It is a proud, sensuous, selfish, luxurious,
church-going, hollow-hearted prosperity.
—Fredric D. Huntington

We are blind—so blind we can't see the blinders that blind us! We are cozier than we think with the norms of the world around us.

Recognize ways the world seeps into your values, and feast on the greater value of being a fellow-citizen with the saints.

FRIDAY
LENT: DAY 21
Reading of the Day: Hebrews 11:1-6

FAST FROM WORRY
FEAST ON FAITH

"The fundamental fact of existence is that this
trust in God, this faith,
is the firm foundation under everything that
makes life worth living.
It's our handle on what we can't see."
Hebrews 11:1-2 The Message

Some days seem especially created for worry. Today
has been one of those days for me! It is good to be
reminded to be very intentional about shelving the
worry and choosing to exercise our faith muscles.
Shelving worry can be a moment-by-moment faith
exercise. Choose to let God grow your faith and
shrink your worry today.

SATURDAY
LENT: DAY 22
Reading of the Day: Acts 20:30-38

FAST FROM SELF-CONDEMNATION
FEAST ON GOD'S WORDS,
"I'VE GOT YOU COVERED!"

"Therefore, there is now no condemnation
for those who are in Christ Jesus."
Romans 8:1

We certainly don't want to take God's forgiveness for granted. But we are guilty of taking His forgiveness lightly if He forgives us, and we, in turn, choose not to forgive ourselves. Take a moment to either sing or reflect on these words from an old hymn:

What can wash away my sin?
Nothing but the blood of Jesus!

His blood truly does cover *all* your sin!

When you stumble, hold out your hand, and let God pull you to your feet again, brush you off, and set you on your way anew.

SUNDAY
HEARTFELT PRAYER
Reading of the Day: Acts 20:30-38

"And being in anguish, he prayed more earnestly,
and his sweat was like drops of blood
falling to the ground."
Luke 22:44

If you have ever taken the Meyers-Briggs personality test, you know one element of the score indicates if you are more of a "thinker" or a "feeler." Whichever you are, follow the examples of Jesus and Paul, and turn your emotions—whether joy or sadness, disappointment, or anticipation—into heartfelt, God-honoring prayers.

The Bible was written in tears,
and to tears it yields its best treasures.
—A. W. Tozer

Oh that there were more crying persons,
when there are so many crying sins!
—Ralph Venning, 17th Century Puritan

MONDAY
LENT: DAY 23
Reading of the Day: Luke 16:10-15

FAST FROM TWO MASTERS
FEAST ON ONE

"No worker can serve two bosses: He'll either hate
the first and love the second
Or adore the first and despise the second. You can't
serve both God and the Bank."
Luke 16:13 The Message

C. S. Lewis wrote, "If you read history you will find that the Christians who did most for the present world were precisely those who thought most of the next. It is since Christians have largely ceased to think of the other world that they have become so ineffective in this."

Who are you serving today?

TUESDAY
LENT: DAY 24
Reading of the Day: I Peter 3:11-17

FAST FROM PRACTICING EVIL
FEAST ON BEING GOOD

I must confess something. I used to find it funny that my Aunt Ruth would always say, "Be good!" or "Be nice!" Looking back, that's a pretty good thing to be remembered for. (My aunt's husband also drove a pink Rambler. Is that cool, or *what?!?*) There's something awfully good about a nice person. I have known of very few people I could characterize as truly *nice*.

(I am not on my short list. I know myself too well!)

Think on this key phrase from the above passage: "Turn from evil and do good."

Now, as my Aunt Ruth used to say,

"BE GOOD!"

WEDNESDAY
LENT: DAY 25
Reading of the Day: Romans 15:1-6

FAST FROM HARSH WORDS
FEAST ON COURTESY

"Finally, all of you be of one mind, having
compassion for one another;
love as brothers, be tenderhearted, be courteous
not returning evil for evil or reviling for reviling,
but on the contrary blessing, knowing
that you were called to this,
that you may inherit a blessing."
I Peter 3:8-9 NKJV

Courtesy is another one of those values that is underrated in today's world. Common courtesy is not so common. The world around us helps us to focus on our own rights. But, is that really a biblical value?

As you go through your day today, remember one key word:

COURTESY

THURSDAY
LENT: 26
Reading of the Day: Proverbs 3:5-8

FAST FROM LEANING
FEAST ON LEANING

No, that is not a typo. Today's admonition is to fast from one kind of leaning and feast on another.

We often kid that we should have named our 115 pound Great Dane, "Ilene." She showed her affection, not with her huge tongue (thankfully!), but by *leaning* her full weight against me.

For years my email signature has been, "Leaning on Him." Don't lean today on your own understanding. Lean on His everlasting arms.

"Trust in the LORD with all your heart and do not
LEAN
on your own understanding."
Proverbs 3:5 NASB

FRIDAY
LENT: DAY 27
Reading of the Day: Mark 9:30-37

FAST FROM LORDING
FEAST ON SERVING

"But they kept silent, for on the way they had
discussed with one another
which of them was the greatest.
Sitting down, He called the twelve and said to them,
'If anyone wants to be first, he shall be
last of all and servant of all.'"
Mark 9:34-35 NASB

There are times I dare to look down my nose on others. My wrong attitudes come across through "one of those looks," tone of voice, behavior, and words. It's easy to fall into the trap of superiority. Some are less wise than I. Some smoke or drink too much—something *I* would never do. Some people's houses are *so* messy. (Mine is not neat, but *is* less messy!) Some people aren't as faithful in their quiet times or don't pray as much as I. There are *many* superiority traps we can fall into. Catch yourself on that today, and feast on a servant's heart instead.

Look back at Mark 9:30-32, and observe what was on Jesus' mind. How does that contrast with the disciples' thoughts?

SATURDAY
LENT: DAY 28
Reading of the Day: Matthew 5:33-37

FAST FROM UNRELIABILITY
FEAST ON KEEPING YOUR WORD

> "But let your statement be, 'Yes, yes' or 'No, no';
> anything beyond these is of evil."
> Matthew 5:37 NASB

In the same vein, attitudes of superiority (from yesterday's fast/feast), you might consider yourself more reliable than others. Sorry, but you are not exempt from today's fast!

Do you ever tell someone you will be praying for them, yet neglect to pray? Take time to think of people you have promised to pray for. Jot down their names in a prominent place, and take time to carry through on your commitment, and pray for them today. Consider writing out a prayer to send them. Or call and ask if you can pray for them over the phone.

What other ways might God be calling on you today to feast on keeping your word?

SUNDAY
SAY "YES" TO "NO!"
Reading of the Day: Mark 8:31-38

> "If anyone wishes to come after me,
> he must deny himself,
> and take up his cross and follow me."
> Mark 8:34 NASB

The 40 days of Lent are intended to be days of preparation, reflection, worship, and self-denial.

Self-denial is not popular. We live in a culture that believes we are entitled to say "yes" to what we want and "no" to anything that imposes on our comfort.

How did Jesus model and teach self-denial in talking with His disciples in the above passage from Mark?

The very act of self-denial can ignite a bonfire of intimacy and worship that is not only important, it's vital. Self-denial does the laundry, the vacuuming, the dusting, the meal preparation, and the candle lighting before the guests ever arrive. Before The Guest arrives. Saying "yes to no" makes room. It vacates our soul of the clutter that occupies needed space. It invites the power of the Holy Spirit to invade.
—Dan Wolgemuth in *Friday Fragments*

MONDAY
LENT: DAY 29
Reading of the Day: Isaiah 40:12-14

FAST FROM THE OBVIOUS
FEAST ON THE UNSEARCHABLE

"Oh, the depth of the riches of the wisdom
and knowledge of God!
How unsearchable his judgments,
and his paths beyond tracing out!"
Romans 11:33

When you walk into a situation today, there will be things that are obvious… who is there, what someone says, even the mood of those present. Ask God to open your eyes to the factors that are *not* obvious. Maybe there is someone who is hurting that might be easily overlooked. Maybe there is a dynamic in relationships that only God's wisdom can reveal. Maybe there is a wise solution that comes only through searching out His wisdom and knowledge.

TUESDAY
LENT: DAY 30
Reading of the Day: Colossians 4:2-6

FAST FROM "WHENEVER"
FEAST ON THE RIGHT MOMENT

"Let your conversation be always full of
grace, seasoned with salt,
so that you may know how [and **when**]
to answer everyone."
Colossians 4:6

We tend (maybe I should say *I* tend) to say what we want, *when* we want. Today I want to challenge you to pick the best moment to really listen to someone rather than throwing in your two bits. Or, if it be a difficult but important subject, pray that God will help you choose the right moment.

Don't let your mouth spout!

WEDNESDAY
LENT: DAY 31
Reading of the Day: I Peter 3:8-16

FAST FROM "HOWEVER"
FEAST ON THE RIGHT WAY

"Always be prepared to give an answer
to everyone who
asks you to give the reason for the
hope that you have."
But do this with gentleness and respect.
I Peter 3:15

This corollary to yesterday's fast and feast can remind you that it's not only important to choose *when* to speak, but *how*. I often pray that God would allow me to properly communicate my thoughts and feelings. Even (or especially) with those we love most, it pays to choose words carefully.

Set a foundation of love, respect, and confidence as the backdrop for difficult words. It sometimes helps to preface your thoughts by saying, "I am not sure how to best express my feelings, so please be patient with me."

THURSDAY
LENT: DAY 32
Reading of the Day: Acts 5:1-11

FAST FROM PART
FEAST ON "ALL"

"That Christ may settle down and
be at home in your hearts by faith."
Ephesians 3:16-17 Weymouth

Have you ever read the little booklet called "My Heart, Christ's Home"? There are many nooks and crannies in our hearts and souls. We gladly invite Christ into our living room or other uncluttered spaces, hoping to keep out of sight the messy closets and "hotspots" that sorely need His attention.

Fast today from those closed closet doors, and let Him shine His light into every corner of your heart, Christ's home.

FRIDAY
LENT: DAY 33
Reading of the Day: Romans 8:5-11

FAST FROM MIND OF FLESH
FEAST ON MIND OF SPIRIT

"The mind of sinful man is death,
but the mind controlled by the
Spirit is life and peace."
Romans 8:6

Characteristics of the mind of the flesh include anxiety, insecurity, fearfulness, sinful desires, resentfulness, and selfishness, among others. These are displeasing to God.

The mind of the Spirit is characterized by consideration of others, Christ-centered thoughts, life, and peace.

Pray today:

*God, give me a heightened awareness
of how I am thinking
and what that thinking is sowing in my heart.
Help me change my thinking,
which can lead to a change in the
way I feel and respond.
Without Your power, I'm powerless to change!*

SATURDAY
LENT: DAY 34
Reading of the Day: II Corinthians 11:21-30

*FAST FROM BOASTING
FEAST ON BOASTING*

"May I never boast except in the cross of
our Lord Jesus Christ,
through which the world has been crucified to me,
and I to the world."
Galatians 6:14

Paul writes again and again of boasting on a human level. In chapter 11 of II Corinthians, he uses the word ten times! The word is used to bring home the idea that any boasting on a human level is worthless. So, if you are going to boast, may you boast in the Lord! What a great God you have, and what great things He has done for you!

What might you tend to boast about today? (Be honest!) Think of a few ways you can boast in the cross of Christ and His strength manifested in your weakness.

SUNDAY
GREAT EXPECTATIONS
Reading of the Day: Philippians 1:20-27

"According to my earnest expectation and hope,
that I may not be put to shame in anything,
but that with all boldness, Christ will…
be exalted in my body."
Philippians 1:20 NASB

Expectations are a funny thing. It's hard to recognize them until they aren't met. Yesterday before a doctor visit, I tried to recognize and then intentionally lower my own expectations. It was only when I left the appointment that I had the sinking feeling of having even my *low* expectations go unmet. I expected at *least* he would listen to what I said I was there for!

As you relate to people today, don't think in terms of what you expect that person will offer you. Instead, try seeing them from the viewpoint of grace.

Re-read Philippians 1:20, and ask God to help you define your own earnest expectations.

MONDAY
LENT: DAY 35
Reading of the Day: II Timothy 2:1-7

FAST FROM DIVISION
FEAST ON MULTIPLICATION

"And the things you have heard me say in the presence of many witnesses entrust to reliable men who will also be qualified to teach others."
II Timothy 2:2

The name of the ministry center where we served in Costa Rica was a mouthful:

Latin America Multiplication Center.

People joked about whether we taught math or if the amazing number of young families with babies on our team were putting multiplication principles into practice! But the purpose of this unwieldy name was to focus on Jesus' ministry model.

We Christians have a well-earned reputation for our skills in division. Fast from division today and feast on multiplication!

TUESDAY
LENT: DAY 36
Reading of the Day: John 14:15-17, 25-27

FAST FROM DISHONESTY
FEAST ON INTEGRITY

"But the Counselor, the Holy Spirit, whom the
Father will send in my name,
will teach you all things and will remind you of
everything I have said to you."
John 14:26

I tend to be honest to a fault. Usually. There are ways that my integrity has cracks. I think we all fall into the same boat. If God's searchlight were to shine on our "integrity," we would lower our heads in shame. Don't let that discourage you today, though! Because, guess what? You have the Helper to make you into a person of integrity!

WEDNESDAY
LENT: DAY 37
Reading of the Day: Deuteronomy 1:15-18

FAST FROM PARTIALITY
FEAST ON UNITY

"For the LORD your God is God of gods and
Lord of lords, the great God, mighty and awesome, who shows no partiality
and accepts no bribes."
Deuteronomy 10:17

God loves all people the same. He shows no partiality. Prejudice is a grievous sin fueled by fear and
ignorance. Prejudice springs from the false notion
that if there are two of us, one must be better than
the other. Ask God today to reveal to you any partiality in your soul. Ask Him to help you reach out
and love those the world shuns. And, while you are
at it, remember that the church is often the seat of
partiality. God calls us to unity, not partiality.

THURSDAY
LENT: DAY 38
Reading of the Day: Proverbs 1:1-9

FAST FROM FOLLY
FEAST ON WISDOM

"The fear of the Lord is the beginning of knowledge;
But fools despise wisdom and discipline."
Proverbs 1:7

My, but it's easy to be a fool! At least for me, it comes naturally. Today let's follow the advice of wise King Solomon. (And let's stick with wisdom to the end of our days, unlike Solomon!) A wise man is teachable. He listens and does not do all the talking. He is not an insufferable know-it-all. Listen to others; listen to Him.

Don't be a fool! Keep this fast/feast in mind throughout your day!

FRIDAY
LENT: DAY 39
Reading of the Day: Philippians 1:3-11

FAST FROM INSINCERITY
FEAST ON AUTHENTICITY

"Being confident of this,
that he who began a good work in you
will carry it on to completion
until the day of Christ Jesus."
Philippians 1:6

The people surrounding you are not expecting perfection. In fact, they see God at work in you and through your own weakness and failure. Though I may not be the world's best mentor, I have learned that those I mentor often learn the most through a humble confession of my own struggles. I intentionally allow them to see how God is working in my areas of weakness, handicaps, and sinfulness.

Give God a chance today to make Himself evident in your life both through the ways He has already changed you, as well as in areas still needing work!

SATURDAY
LENT: DAY 40 (LAST DAY!)
Reading of the Day: II Timothy 2:20-26

FAST FROM IMPURITY
FEAST ON HOLINESS

"Flee the evil desires of youth and pursue
righteousness, faith, love, and peace,
along with those who call on the
Lord out of a pure heart."
II Timothy 2:22

Holiness is not a commonly heard word today, even in Christian circles. Yet we are commanded, "Be holy, for I am holy."

Holiness is a tough concept to wrap our brains around, but it's a quality emphasized time and again in Scripture. Jesus stressed holiness in His teaching. The epistles also clearly teach us to flee immorality and maintain purity. It's a concept the world scoffs at today, but perhaps for that very reason, we should hold onto it all the tighter!

Ask God right now how He would have you fast from impurity and feast on holiness today.

EASTER SUNDAY
HE IS RISEN!
Reading of the Day: Luke 24:1-12

HE IS RISEN, INDEED!

The subject of the resurrection usually comes up only at Easter or when a believer dies. For most people in the world, "Jesus rose from the dead," has as much importance as, "Hannibal crossed the Alps."

It is obvious that the story of the empty tomb cannot be fitted into our contemporary worldview, or indeed into any worldview except one of which it is the starting point.
—Lesslie Newbigin

The resurrection of Christ changed everything, and there is no going back.

Where is your hope found today? Make a conscious choice (aloud in prayer, if possible) to pin all your hope on Jesus, His life, and transforming resurrection. Allow the mystery of Easter to turn your life right side up and remind you of the foundation upon which your hope is built.

Appendix B:
Advent

As an amateur writer, I admit I am guilty of using too many exclamation points! However, the story of the Messiah coming to earth deserves one big exclamation point. So here it is:

!

As we walk through the Bible during these days of Advent (which means to look forward to the coming Messiah), some of the passages we will explore talk of people in Jesus' lineage who were key characters in God's preparation for the coming of His Son. My hope and desire is that by the time you reach December 25th in this calendar, you will be looking forward to the celebration of our Messiah even more than anticipating the gifts and turkey. (It's OK to enjoy the gifts and turkey with a thankful heart!)

ADVENT
DAY ONE
CULTURAL REPROACH
Reading of the Day: Luke 1:1-7

Over the next weeks, join me on a spiritual journey towards the celebration of Jesus' birth.

Elizabeth was the mother of John the Baptist, who would prepare the way for the Messiah, even as the prophets foretold. In the times of Zechariah and Elizabeth, the lack of children not only deprived them of personal joy and fulfillment, but also brought the reproach of their society, as barrenness was considered a sign of God's disfavor. There are many indications of this throughout the scriptures, such as the stories of Sarai, Rebekah, Rachel, and Hannah.

In the midst of her shame, Elizabeth obviously found her sufficiency in God alone. I can just picture her in her emotional pain, crying out the words of the Psalmist:

"My soul thirsts for God, for the living God.
When can I go and meet with God?
Why are you downcast, O my soul?
Put your hope in God, for I will yet praise him,
my Savior and my God!"
(Excerpts from Psalm 42)

Make these words your own heart's cry today as we begin this Advent season.

ADVENT
DAY TWO
IT'S A BOY!
Reading of the Day: Luke 1:8-17

IT'S A BOY!
NAME: JOHN
PROUD PARENTS:
ZACHARIAH AND ELIZABETH
WEIGHT: ABOUT THAT
OF A NEWBORN LAMB

WE HAVE JOY AND GLADNESS, AND YOU
ARE INVITED TO JOIN US IN REJOICING
AT HIS BIRTH. (Luke 1:14)

HE WILL BE GREAT IN THE SIGHT OF
THE LORD. (v.15a)
HE HAS BEEN FILLED WITH THE HOLY
SPIRIT SINCE CONCEPTION (v. 15b)
(*NOT THAT WE'RE BRAGGING!*)

HE IS THE FORERUNNER OF THE
MESSIAH—WITH THE SPIRIT AND
POWER OF ELIJAH (v. 17)
(For more details, check with Luke!)

ADVENT
DAY THREE
TRADITION!
Reading of the Day: Luke 1:57-66

"[Zechariah] asked for a writing tablet, and to
everyone's astonishment he wrote,
'His name is John.'"
Luke 1:63

In the musical, *Fiddler on the Roof*, Tevye sings
passionately about the importance of tradition in
Jewish society. The roots of tradition went deep in
the times of Elizabeth and Zechariah. Back then the
firstborn child was traditionally named after the father or grandfather. When Elizabeth and Zechariah
both confirmed that their long-awaited son would
be named "John," it's no wonder the people were
astounded!

In our culture, when a baby is named, the significance of the name is sometimes considered.
However, more often than not, it's just a name that
sounds good at that point in history. But I ask you
today to reflect on the shock waves that echoed
throughout the community when Zechariah's
tongue was finally loosened upon declaring that his
son's name would be *JOHN!*

ADVENT
DAY FOUR
IS IT POSSIBLE?
Reading of the Day: Luke 1:28-37

"Nothing is impossible with God." Luke 1:37

Do you recall the context of the above verse? These words were spoken by Gabriel to Mary. She was called on in a BIG WAY to cling to those words! In today's passage we see many declarations which required leaps of faith on Mary's part. We'll look at just two today:

1) Gabriel's greeting challenged her to believe she was highly favored, and God was with her. (Think on that a minute. Do you ever have a hard time believing God highly values *you*?)

2) Then she was told, "Don't be afraid." That, in and of itself required trust, didn't it? Just seeing an angel gave great cause for fear!

God is with you. Know that you are indeed favored by God and need not fear.

ADVENT
DAY FIVE
LEAPS OF FAITH
Reading of the Day: Luke 1:28-37

We are going to continue to focus on this portion of Luke 1 for three more days. As you re-read it today, look for other leaps of faith taken by Mary that day. Here are some I've noted—from Mary's perspective:

- I am not dreaming.

- Miracles *can* happen!

- My son, out of all sons, will save Israel. He will be called the Son of the Most High. (Wow! The Messiah. The very *Son of God!*)

- As poor as I am, my son will become a king.

- Elizabeth is going to have a baby also, and she is far beyond child-bearing years!

Nothing. Nothing is impossible for God. Take a time-out in your busy December, and do a soul-check. Is there something in your life that seems impossible? Put that "something" in God's hands.

ADVENT
DAY SIX
BUT HOW?
Reading of the Day: Luke 1:28-37
(Read from The Message, if you can)

"But how? I've never slept with a man."
Luke 1:34

Keep thinking today about Mary's challenge to believe the impossible. The term "virgin" in those days not only implied the obvious, but probably referred to girls age 14 and under.

I can picture Mary and her friends playing out the Old Testament stories, like Hannah's promise to have a son in her old age. I suspect Mary knew by heart Hannah's words of praise upon receiving God's promise. In the culture of the times, girls longed to be wives and mothers. But this news?!? Mary, a virgin, was to become a mother! And not only that. Her son was to be the Son of God Almighty Himself. The King of kings, whose kingdom would never end.

Mary and her people would have longed for the Messiah. Though Mary's heart responded in trust, her mind wondered, "But HOW?"

ADVENT
DAY SEVEN
CALLED ON TO BELIEVE
Reading of the Day: Once more…Luke 1:28-37

When Zechariah questioned the angel, he was made mute. When Mary asked a similar question, she received an answer. Obviously, her response was not questioning IF God could do this, but HOW this would happen. She'd already trusted the God of the Impossible by believing she would bear a son… not only *that*, but the Son of the Almighty! *Now* she was called on to accept by faith the answer to her question.

> "The Holy Spirit will come upon you, and the power of the Most High will overshadow you."
> Luke 1:35

That answer required even *more* faith! Let's review what Mary had been called upon to believe:

- That she was not dreaming

- That she would bear a son as a virgin

- That He would be the Son of the Most High

- That miracles do happen

- That her son would be the King of Kings

- That her relative Elizabeth would bear a son in her old age

- That she would become pregnant through the shadow of the Most High coming upon her

Can you think of anything else Mary was called on to believe? What is God calling on *you* to believe today?

ADVENT
DAY EIGHT
SAY AGAIN?!?
Reading of the Day: John 19:24-30

God gave Mary a very important gift by giving her a crystal clear message through an unforgettable messenger. Gabriel made very clear God's promise, telling her that:

- He will be great and will be called the Son of the Most High.

- The Lord God will give him the throne of his father David.

- And He will reign... his kingdom will never end.

- So the holy one to be born will be called the Son of God.

(excerpts from Luke 1:32-35)

After the angel left her, perhaps Mary had to pinch herself. She could have had cause to doubt. "Did the angel say that he'd be the Son of God, or did I just misunderstand?"

I believe God gave Mary the gift of the angel's clear words stated in several ways so that in the challenging days and years to come Mary could cling to that experience—*even* as He hung on the cross.

ADVENT
DAY NINE
EARTHLY PROOF OF HEAVENLY
CERTAINTY
Reading of the Day: Luke 1:18-25

When our faith is stretched, it seems that often God challenges us to step just a bit further from our comfort zones. We've seen how Mary was called upon to believe that, "Nothing is impossible with God." I have to almost laugh as we look at the last impossibility she's called on to believe. Gabriel offered this as proof of God's ability: "Even Elizabeth your relative is going to have a child in her old age." If God could overshadow Mary and cause her to conceive His very own Son, it seems a no-brainer that He could cause an older, barren woman to conceive a child with an earthly father.

Maybe the other declarations of the angel were

bigger tests of faith, but the tangible evidence of Elizabeth's pregnancy would be the earthly proof of heaven's certainty: God is the Master of the impossible!

ADVENT
DAY TEN
SPOUT VS. SPROUT
Reading of the Day: Genesis 1:21-28

"Who would have said to Abraham that Sarah
would nurse children?
Yet I have borne him a son in his old age."
—Sarah in Genesis 21:7

In preface to reading Mary's Song later in Luke 1, let's get a bit of context. The Jewish people in Mary's day were very familiar with the Old Testament stories. Among those was the story of Sarah. Surely Mary remembered the laughter of Sarah, who miraculously conceived long after she was considered barren. She must have thought about that upon pondering the news of Elizabeth conceiving a child.

Mary's mind was obviously filled with the words of the law and prophets. She certainly did *not* **spout** a spiritual response or simply mouth words she recalled from the scriptures. Instead, I think her godly response **sprouted** from her deep spiritual grounding.

ADVENT
DAY ELEVEN
LET'S SEE WHAT SPILLS
Reading of the Day: I Samuel 25:12-24

Yesterday we looked at one woman whom Mary likely admired. Today we read another biblical account of a wise woman who modeled Mary's own response. When Abigail was faced with the destruction of her home and family, she wisely approached David's men, saying, "Here is your maidservant, ready to serve you."

When we read Mary's Magnificat, we will see Mary using many phrases from her biblical heroes. She was so familiar with women in the history of her people (like Abigail) who responded in wise, godly ways, that her natural (and perhaps supernatural) response mirrored theirs.

I've often thought of the example of a full glass of liquid. If you were to carry that glass and someone bumped into you, what would spill? What are you carrying in your glass today? If you are "bumped," what would spill?

ADVENT
DAY TWELVE
HE LEAPED!
Reading of the Day: Luke 1:39-45

How happy Mary and Elizabeth must have been to see one another after their respective divine experiences! Mary was possibly two months along in her pregnancy when they met up, but Elizabeth's baby had already been active for weeks. When she saw Mary, however, the baby within Elizabeth didn't just kick or move. He LEAPED! Little John made it very clear that this "meeting of the wombs" was an extraordinary event!

John was obviously filled with the Spirit, even before his birth. His ears were so tuned to God, he heard the voice of his Savior's mother before his ears were fully formed.

As Elizabeth's son leaped within her, these marvelous words leaped from her mouth,

> "Blessed are you among women,
> and blessed is the child that you will bear!"

ADVENT
DAY THIRTEEN
THE GREATNESS OF THE LIFE WITHIN
Reading of the Day: Deuteronomy 32:7, Leviticus 19:32, I Timothy 5:1,2

"Blessed is she who has believed that what the Lord has said to her will be accomplished!"
Luke 1:45

In biblical times there was a much greater respect for elders than in today's society. The reading of the day includes a few of many passages from the Bible that clearly teach such respect. We see the tables were turned when we read of Elizabeth's response to her younger relative, Mary:

"But why am I so favored, that the mother of my Lord should come to me?"
Luke 1:43

It was quite a change of hats for Elizabeth to say she was undeserving of even Mary's presence. It wasn't so much Mary's greatness; it was the greatness of the life within her.

Elizabeth was so in tune with God, she immediately recognized the enormity of faith required to believe all that the Lord had spoken to Mary.

ADVENT
DAY FOURTEEN
UNUSUAL "WOMEN'S TALK"
Reading of the Day: Luke 1:46-55

"Blessed are you among women,
and blessed is the child you will bear!"
—Elizabeth

"My soul glorifies the Lord
And my spirit rejoices in God my Savior."
—Mary

Mary and Elizabeth explored the depths of spiritual communion and mutual encouragement. How I would love to jump back in time and be present during that precious encounter where Elizabeth and Mary glorified God!

I'm afraid if I were in Elizabeth's sandals when Mary arrived, my first words would have been, "Can you believe that at my age I'm actually pregnant?!?"

Even worse, I can imagine myself in Mary's sandals saying, "Wow! The trip here was exhausting, and I've never felt so nauseated. Have *you* had morning sickness?"

I thank God for Mary's Magnificat. What an example to us of how we should glorify God; how we should know His Word inside out!

ADVENT
DAY FIFTEEN
COMPOSING A DIVINE SONG
Reading of the Day: Psalm 71:19-24, Micah 7:18

"For the Mighty One has done great things for
me—holy is His name!"
Luke 1:49

Mary's poetic outburst in Luke 1 is often called
the "Magnificat," meaning "glorifying." The word
comes from Mary's first phrase, "My soul glorifies
the Lord." The song celebrates the greatness of God.

There are many parallels with Old Testament passages which we will look at in coming days. I believe Mary had stored in her memory many of these
Scriptures. But no human being could just "string
together" phrases from various Biblical sources. I
believe the Holy Spirit used what was guarded in
Mary's heart to compose one of the most divine
songs ever recorded in history. The words of Psalm
71 and Micah 7 are similar to Mary's thoughts in
Luke 1:49

"Your righteousness reaches to the skies, O God,
You who have done great things.
Who, O God, is like you?"
Psalm 71:19

ADVENT
DAY SIXTEEN
THE BABY'S PEDIGREE
Reading of the Day: Micah 5:1-5

St. Francis of Assisi set up the first crèche in 1223, with the purpose of turning people's focus back to the birth of Christ rather than materialism and the giving of gifts. (It's hard to imagine the pressures of Christmas back in the 13th century!) The purpose of this Advent calendar is much the same as St. Francis of Assisi's: to prioritize Christ in the midst of the season's hustle and bustle.

Let's set the stage for the nativity scene we will be reflecting on in the coming days.

> "In those days Caesar Augustus issued a decree
> that a census should be taken of the
> entire Roman world."
> Luke 2:7

Luke is the only gospel writer who relates his narrative to dates of world history. He gives mention of Caesar Augustus, the first and possibly the greatest, Roman emperor. God used the decree of a pagan emperor to fulfill the prophecy of Micah 5:2.

As Charles Spurgeon put it, "The official stamp of the Roman Empire shall be affixed to the pedigree of the coming Son of David, and Bethlehem shall behold his nativity."

ADVENT
DAY SEVENTEEN
THE MANGER AND THE CROSS
Reading of the Day: Isaiah 53:1-6

As we continue to set the scene for the crèche, let's look at some reasons why God chose to have Joseph and Mary lay the baby Messiah in a manger.

This humble birthplace showed his humiliation. He came to be "despised and rejected by mankind, a man of suffering and familiar with pain." "He had no beauty or majesty to attract us." Would it have been fitting that the man who was to die naked on the cross should be robed in purple at his birth?

Charles Spurgeon wrote, "Would it not have been inappropriate that the Redeemer who was to be buried in a borrowed tomb should be born anywhere but in the humblest shed, and housed anywhere but in the most ignoble manner? The manger and the cross standing at the two extremities of the Savior's earthly life seem most fit and congruous the one to the other."

"Foxes have dens, and birds have nests, but the Son of Man has no place to lay his head."
Matthew 8:20

Nothing could be more fitting in the baby's season of humiliation than the manger. He laid aside all his glory, took up the form of a servant, and humbled himself to the meanest estate—to be laid in a manger.

ADVENT
DAY EIGHTEEN
THE DONKEY KNOWS
Reading of the Day: Isaiah 1:2-4, 16-20

Now that the scene is set for the manger, let's add our first figure—an unlikely one! If you are setting up your own crèche as we progress, I doubt you'll find this first animal in your collection.

Donkeys generally can't talk, though Balaam could tell you of a time one did. (Numbers 22:30) The ox and the donkey have a lot to teach us.

> "The ox knows his master,
> The donkey his owner's manger,
> But Israel does not know,
> My people do not understand."
> Isaiah 1:3

While the shepherds and the wise men were *told* where to find the manger, the donkey knew on his own. Let's not be like the people of Israel who were soon to reject the incarnation of the Messiah. Let's be like the humble donkey and know our Master.

ADVENT
DAY NINETEEN
MARY HAD A LITTLE LAMB
Reading of the Day: I Peter 1:17-21

Let's add a sheep or two to the manger scene today. We know for sure that shepherds came to worship the newborn King. I can only imagine that they brought their sheep in tow! When Jesus began his ministry, John the Baptist would proclaim,

> "Look, the Lamb of God,
> who takes away the sin of the world!"
> John 1:29

The newborn Savior would present himself as the perfect, unblemished Lamb to be sacrificed in order to fulfill all the righteous requirements of the Law. This perfect Lamb would reconcile many to God, once and for all.

One day heavenly voices would sing,

> "Worthy is the Lamb, who was slain,
> to receive power and wealth
> and wisdom and strength
> and honor and glory and praise!"
> Rev. 5:12

Today the Nativity lamb invites you to rehearse with the heavenly choir.

ADVENT
DAY TWENTY
MOOVE!
Reading of the Day: II Chronicles 5:2-6;
Hebrews 10:8-10

"We have been made holy through the sacrifice of
the body of Jesus Christ once for all."
Hebrews 10:10

Let's add a cow to the Nativity scene today. The cow has a lot of reason to "moo" with delight, while chewing its cud at the baby's side. Remember the overwhelming scene of sacrifice as Solomon and a vast crowd brought the Ark to the Temple, "sacrificing so many sheep and cattle that they could not be recorded or counted."

Now with the birth of the Messiah, no more cows would need to be sacrificed! A tiny baby in a manger perhaps was not a breath-taking sight, especially compared with Solomon's procession. Through the cow's eyes, however, we can recognize that the suffering and death of this baby boy would have an impact far above and beyond the animal sacrifices.

Just this thought ought to MOOve you to praise God!

ADVENT
DAY TWENTY-ONE
CLOSE TO THE SHEPHERD'S HEART
Reading of the Day: Luke 2:8-20

"He tends his flock like a shepherd:
He gathers the lambs in his arms and carries them
close to his heart."
Isaiah 40:11

How glorious is the story of the shepherds and the huge angelic choir! How I would have loved to join them in that field, "~~washing their socks by night~~" —oh, sorry!—"watching their flocks by night." The humble shepherds received the most important birth announcement in history.

We've looked at a number of figures that *might* have been present at the original manger. But we know for *certain* the shepherds went and saw him firsthand. That baby would grow up to become the Good Shepherd (John 10:14), the Chief Shepherd (I Peter 5:4), the Great Shepherd (Hebrews 13:20), and the One Shepherd (John 10:16).

What was the shepherds' response after seeing the Baby Messiah with their very own eyes? The same responses we should have today:

1. "They spread the word concerning what had been told them about this child."

2. They returned, "…glorifying and praising God for all the things they had heard and seen."

ADVENT
DAY TWENTY-TWO
WE THREE KINGS
Reading of the Day: Matthew 2:1-12

Note a couple of interesting details regarding the kings we add to the manger scene today.

- The kings visited "the child," probably at least a few months after his birth.

- The child was "*born a king*," he was not born to *become* a king.

- At least three times in this account Matthew writes, "the child and his mother" instead of "the mother and her child," as one would customarily note. They bowed at *his* feet, they worshiped *him*, and they presented their gifts to *him*.

- The traditional manger scenes include "three kings," representing the magi who brought 1) gold, 2) frankincense, and 3) myrrh—gifts which were also presented to

King Solomon. No one knows how many "kings" came from the east… we can only count the number of gifts mentioned.

I have recently been taken by the words of "We Three Kings." The song speaks more of The King than the three who visited him.

> *Glorious now behold Him arise,*
> *King and God and Sacrifice.*
> *Alleluia, alleluia!*
> *Sounds through the earth and skies.*

ADVENT
DAY TWENTY-THREE
THE UNSPOKEN HERO
Reading of the Day: Matthew 1:18-25; 2:13-15

In the days of Jesus, it was the cultural norm for the father of the groom to approach the bride's father. If the fathers agreed to the marriage, the groom paid a price—a sort of reverse dowry. The couple then exchanged vows and were legally married, but did not live together for a year.

Adding Joseph to the crèche, we see a righteous man, married to his pregnant bride. If he did not divorce her, he would be admitting that the child was his own. (*"Isn't this the carpenter's son?"* Matthew 13:55) Joseph was not only righteous but also kind.

He planned to divorce her secretly, and would thus lose the dowry he had paid. Not only did he humble himself to pay the price for his bride, he then listened to the angel (more than once) and obeyed immediately, giving up everything for his bride and her son.

During Jesus' life on earth, he reflected the image of his true Father. But we also see in Jesus the example lived out by his earthly father—an obedient man who willingly took on the shame of an unfaithful bride (us!) and paid her price anyway, because of his sacrificial love for her.

ADVENT
DAY TWENTY-FOUR
THE EMPTY MANGER
Reading of the Day:
Mark 1:40-41 and John 13:1-5

In Latin America, the arrangement of the nativity scene is a very important ritual.

Tradition dictates that the manger remain empty until Christmas Eve. When the children awake Christmas morning, they *might* look for their shoes to be filled with treats from the Christ Child (now sadly being replaced by Santa), but they will *surely* look at the crèche and marvel that the manger now holds the newborn baby King. Now, that's the focus we strive for!

See the baby's hands? These hands would be strong enough to turn over the merchant's tables, yet tender enough to touch the leper's rotting flesh and make him whole. These hands would not be afraid to take the disciples' dusty, dirty feet and wash them. These hands would willingly receive the spikes to hold Him to the cross as He paid the price for you and me.

ADVENT
DAY TWENTY-FIVE
SPEAKING OF THE DEVIL...
Reading of the Day: I Peter 5:6-11

Today we have another unlikely figure, unless you've lived in Mexico. There, lurking in the background, is a small figure dressed in red. Satan, who is always present in a Mexican *nacimiento*, is there to remind us that although the birth of Jesus offers love and the possibility of redemption, sin and evil are always present in the world. The Redeemer came down from heaven into a sinful world because this evil world and we fallen people desperately needed a Savior.

In the weeks preceding Christmas, people are often generous, courteous, and helpful. Today that is likely not so. With the final pressures of gift buying and grocery shopping (often compounded with icy streets), people push their way to the front of the line, grab the last item off the shelf in front of you, and blast their horn when your tires are spinning.

Today when someone shows you anything but the Christmas spirit, remember the red figure prowling in the background of our world. Let that be a gentle reminder of the significance of the Baby's birth.

ADVENT
DAY TWENTY-SIX
BEHIND THE SCENES
Reading of the Day: Matthew 10:26-31

I have never seen a carved wooden sparrow in a creche. But, don't you imagine there were one or two looking on in the manger scene?

There are several remarkably unremarkable characteristics of sparrows. Rarely has anyone cried out, "Oh, look! There's a sparrow!" Their gray and brown plumage is dull and unnoticeable. They are called the "common sparrow" for the very reason that they are ubiquitous. * Even the unassuming sparrow evidences God's creativity, from its ritual of "dirt baths" to its impressive average flight speed over 28 mph with wings beating 15 times a second!

The humble sparrow today looks down on the baby in the manger. This same Jesus would one day look up and say, "So, don't be afraid. You are worth more than many sparrows."

*Eight pair of them were originally introduced to the US by the British in 1851. They were, however, native to the Mediterranean area at the time of Christ.

ADVENT
DAY TWENTY-SEVEN
COME, LET US WORSHIP
AND BOW DOWN
Reading of the Day: Isaiah 9:6-7;
Philippians 2:5-11

Go, tell it on the mountain, that Jesus Christ is born!

Mary and Joseph followed the angel's instructions and named the baby "Jesus," which means "Savior." He would bear many names in His life. We must marvel at the culmination of the Advent season, adding the final, chief figure to our crèche—the baby called:

"Wonderful Counselor, *Almighty God.*"

The shepherds and wise men bowed before the infant and child at the beginning of his life. Philippians 2 paints a clear picture of how Jesus humbled himself by taking the form of a helpless

One. This baby grew up to be a man who would suffer and die for us. Thankfully, the Christmas story doesn't end there! God also highly exalted him, so that not only shepherds and magi would bow before him, but

> "That at the name of Jesus
> **every knee should bow**…
> And every tongue acknowledge that
> Jesus Christ is Lord
> To the glory of God the Father."

Take time to bow before him today, acknowledging him as Lord.

CPSIA information can be obtained
at www.ICGtesting.com
Printed in the USA
LVHW02s2331151018
593746LV00001B/9/P